CAN'T
NOT
DO

CAN'T
NOT
DO

The Compelling Social Drive That
CHANGES OUR WORLD

Paul Shoemaker

WILEY

*Lori, Ben, Nick, and Sam, there is no way I am the person
I am without each of you and all of you.*

CONTENTS

PROLOGUE: THE POWER OF CAN'T NOT DO

I remember everything and nothing about August 9, 2013. I was sitting in a Seattle coffee shop when an e-mail flashed into my inbox. It was from a *Wall Street Journal* reporter I'd never heard of, asking if I knew anything about "the person whose plane had just crashed in East Haven, Connecticut." I had no idea what the reporter was talking about and assumed he had the wrong guy. I reread it just to be sure and hit delete.

Moments later, my phone rang. Through a flood of tears, my friend Susan asked me not talk to any media or answer their calls. Then she told me why. After she hung up, the next flood of tears was down my face. I prayed, desperate for some miracle, any miracle, but I knew the truth. I actually knew a lot about the person whose plane had crashed. Susan had just lost her remarkable husband and her beautiful son. Another family, on the ground, had lost their two wonderful young girls with their whole lives ahead of them. And we all lost a damn good man.

That damn good man was Bill Henningsgaard. He had spent the first 20 years of his career building sales and international channels at Microsoft; he was universally respected. But he'd be the first to tell you that job was really just preparation for becoming a community leader, a catalyst, and an agent for positive social change in the fullest sense. He was the real deal. I had last spoken to Bill, my good friend and role model, just a few days before he and his 18-year-old son, Max, took off to visit colleges. He was one of the first people I interviewed for this book when I was trying to digest and distill, at a pretty casual pace at first, what I had been learning through the past 17 years of my work.

I had been planning to take the lessons of people like Bill, inspiring nonprofit leaders, social innovators, philanthropists, and committed citizens, and share those stories in a way in which millions more could see themselves and find that deeper commitment to their community. It is no exaggeration to say that this tragedy steeled my resolve and commitment. I'd been mulling this over, thinking about writing a book, but my sense of urgency was given a jolt, albeit for the worst possible reason.

I was asked to be one of the eulogists at Bill's service a week later. More than 1,000 people attended the service. I will never forget walking up to the lectern and turning around to see all of those faces and feeling all that shared pain. I took a few moments and just stood silent to look around the room and take it in. I got the courage to even breathe the first word because of what I felt emanating from the whole room: a shared, profound sense of sadness and loss we were all feeling together. And I felt one more thing . . .

. . . a deep desire to share just a little of what I had learned about Bill and the kind of human being he was. In those gut-wrenching days after 8/9/13, dozens of people sent me notes about Bill, sharing how they felt about him and their reflections on him. One word was used numerous times, not a word commonly used to describe a person, but Bill was an uncommon person. That word was beacon. One of its dictionary definitions is simply, "Someone that guides or gives hope to others" . . . yep, that was Bill. It hurts writing these words right now.

I asked Susan if it was okay to share Bill's story like this. She told me, "Absolutely! Sharing Bill's story, how he found his path and belief in the need for everyone to contribute, might help create the kind of world we hope to live in." You'll hear more about my friend, Bill, later, but his life, and even the loss of him, galvanized my personal mission in a way I never expected. Now, I can't not be a messenger and share these stories and their collective wisdom. I can't not share what I've seen, heard, and lived from walking alongside all the people you'll read about here. I can't not use what I've learned to guide others, perhaps people like you, who feel the urge to do more for the world and to translate that impulse into action.

Can't Not Do—The Social Drive That Changes the World

I can't not do this.

It's not that I can do this, it's that I can't not.

I don't have time to not make an impact.

I could not imagine not.

I don't remember the first time I heard someone use one of these grammatically incorrect phrases. But I hear these statements consistently, to this day, from educated and literate people. I know you have heard of "can-do" people, they are eager and willing, we admire them and hope our children become like them when they grow up. But the regular heroes you will meet in this book go way beyond can-do, they *can't not do.*

These people make a decision at some point in their lives that there is something, some burning cause, in their world that they have to do something about. That they can't not do something about, like kindergarten readiness, leadership development, homelessness, environmental challenges, board governance, youth violence, and so many others. Sometimes the cause is a social issue, but it might also be some expertise or personal passion you want to leverage for good in the world. There is a reason, a power, in why they all said something like can't not do. These people have found a cause that grabbed them and won't let go. They may face indecision and uncertainty many times along their journey, after all, they are regular people, not superheroes. But they dig deeper for answers, sometimes unconventional, and ultimately find the conviction and dedication to jump in for the long run.

Some of these people have made a career change to commit their lives to their cause, while others have decided they could find and dedicate a few extra hours a week within their busy schedules. Some people bring money to the equation. Some bring street smarts and know-how. Some bring time and motivation. Some bring innovation. Some are willing to connect with others, to go to hard places to find root causes and be humbled in the process. There are many different routes and ways people create change once they have found their can't not do (Appendix 3 might help you).

Can't not do is a catchphrase I'm using to capture the essence, the heart, of these people and their choices in a unique and, I hope, memorable way. It's the framing for the stories I want to share with you. I am beyond passionate, *almost desperate*, to tell these peoples' stories and what I've learned from more than a decade and a half of day-in, day-out interaction.

I started sharing parts of this book with a few friends. After I sent a draft to my friend, Jim Pitofksy, he called his wife, Becky. She said something he hadn't heard her say before, but he liked it. Way back before they got engaged, her mom apparently told Becky, "Don't marry the guy you think you can live with. Marry the guy you think you can't live without."

As I started sending out drafts to friends to get their feedback, I kept getting more comments like that, using that double negative syntax in one form or another. Some of them told me that phrasing an idea or question in that way makes it stickier, more memorable, visceral, harder to dismiss.

I've been so privileged to work at the intersection between philanthropically minded people and nonprofit change agents—a truly unique vantage point, down the street and around the world. My experiences are real-time, nothing theoretical or from a research lab. I've worked very hard over the past year to distill all those years and people and experiences, successes and failures into this one book to share with each of you who is ready to dig in deeper and more intentionally to help create positive change in your community and world.

As I've talked and worked with more and more of these regular heroes, I have realized that they share some fundamental beliefs about the world, possess some common "readinesses" and, over time, have learned some of the same lessons. This book developed out of these commonalities and my experiences, and I believe it can help you translate your ideas and can't-not-do impulses into action that betters our world.

This is not, repeat *not*, a self-help book; it's a help-the-world book. If this helps you feel better, and it probably should, that's a nice-to-have side benefit. For me, if this book ends up helping you live a happier, healthier life, that's good, but that's ultimately a means to an end. At the end of the day, I don't care as much about helping you *feel* better for *yourself* as I do empowering you to *do* better for *the world* around you.

This is a how-to book for people who want to help change the world, a street-readiness dialogue between you and me and you and your inner aspirations. Just in case you think I am some turtleneck-wearing, bongo-drum-beating, bleeding heart, woo-woo guru, I'm not. This is on the ground, in the trenches, real world. It's messy, human work, full of as many failures as successes. These are authentic stories, vital questions, and unconventional answers that can guide and inspire each of us to realize our fullest potential to create positive social change.

Trees and Labs

On Earth Day 1970, Andy Lipkis went from being your typical 15-year-old Los Angeles teen to a tree-loving activist. By the time he turned 18, he had founded TreePeople (www.treepeole.org) and was already organizing tree-planting parties that put thousands of seedlings in the ground around Los Angeles. Eleven years later, for the 1984 Los Angeles Olympics, he spearheaded the planting of one million trees as a symbolic and tangible way of absorbing pollution in the city. Not one thousand, one *million* trees. He started with little more than his passion, but 40 years later, he still heads up the organization, now an environmental leader. I first met Andy in 1988. There was something about how deeply committed he was to this cause. I had never met anyone quite like him. He was unique in his energy, his single-focused, sustained drive. He was a regular guy . . . but then again, he wasn't.

Seventeen years later, I met Suzi Levine. In some ways, Suzi is a regular gal . . . but then again, she isn't. She can be a hurricane of energy and began focusing that energy with two brain researchers who were tucked away in a building on the corner of the University of Washington campus. She thought the findings of these researchers could change thousands, maybe millions, of young lives and was not willing to let that opportunity languish without doing what she could to contribute.

Patricia Kuhl and Andy Meltzoff at the Institute for Learning & Brain Sciences (I-LABS),[1] the world's first brain-imaging facility focused on children, were learning that the amount of brain development in the first five years of life is astounding. About 85 percent of brain development happens between birth and five years of age, and that percent often shapes a child's success in life. They also knew that, in the United States, one-third of children show up for their first day of kindergarten two years behind, developmentally. That almost-incomprehensible gap is what the researchers were working to close, but it wasn't going to get done in academic journals; they had to get their findings and expertise out to the public and into the hands of parents and schools. That's what Suzi began helping to do in a powerful way (we'll revisit Suzi in more detail in Chapter 6). Like Andy, there was something compelling about how deeply committed Suzi was to this cause.

Andy and Suzi are not unique in our world. There are others out there, regular heroes making a significant impact on some of our most intractable social issues. And you probably have never heard of them. Most people making significant change in our world are not famous like Bono or Angelina Jolie or Bill and Melinda Gates. Andy and Suzi are regular people like you and me, like millions of people who want to help change our world. They are regular heroes and they have a overwhelming passion for impacting their community for the better.

There are some big problems in our world. To most of us, they seem so large and impassable that we find it hard to imagine a way forward. But, time and time again, we increasingly see regular people making a difference, sometimes *the* difference. It might look like they are tilting at windmills. The problems are complex, the politics are murky, and the players innumerable. Yet, there are people who take personal responsibility for tackling the issues. In Andy's case, it would become his life's work. For Suzi, it was what she could fit in alongside her professional career. In both cases, success came from committed action arising from a deep personal drive.

The World Does Not Lack Solutions

We know how to solve the majority of the world's most difficult social problems. This is the surprising truth: we already have proven solutions to most of our social challenges. I not only believe this, I've watched it play out in schools, neighborhoods, and communities as the founding president of Social Venture Partners International, a global network of thousands of social innovators, philanthropists, entrepreneurs, and business and community leaders that fund and support social change in nearly 40 cities in eight countries around the world (www.socialventurepartners.org). I am convinced that coming up with more solutions to our problems is not our world's greatest challenge, although we do need innovation. Nor is it finding more money for social change, although that always helps.

What we need most is more human and social capital. Simply put, more people committed for the long-term to making a change.

We need more people in the game, committing to that one cause, that one challenge where they feel they can make a real dent. History has proved that if enough people hammer away long enough at a social problem, we start to change our world for the better. And the amount of positive change one human being can help create today has never been greater. Take Jeff Carr, for example, who helped prove a solution existed to a social problem many at the time thought hopeless.

Jeff Carr grew up in Seattle, but he took off for college to see what more was out there in the world. He chose a physical education major with dreams of becoming a professional soccer player. In his sophomore year of college in the mid-1980s, he took a trip to Portugal's Azores Islands with an all-star team and saw first-hand what was out there in the world. He saw poverty like he'd never seen in his life, and it shook him to his core. When he got back to school, he changed his major to philosophy and religion.

After graduating, he spent the next 20 years involved in urban ministries and directing youth centers in Los Angeles. In 2006, when most forms of crime were falling in Los Angeles and violent crime was decreasing all over the United States, gang-related homicides, robberies, and assaults spiked about 15 percent higher in Los Angeles.[2] It was a lightning bolt issue, a flash point for the city, and for Jeff. To stop the violence, Mayor Antonio Villaraigosa wanted to appoint a gang czar to oversee the city's gang reduction and youth development programs. The mayor didn't have to look far. There was Jeff, with his extensive background working in some of Los Angeles's toughest neighborhoods.

I met Jeff on a trip to L.A. in 2012. Andy Lipkis actually connected us. I had lived in Los Angeles in the late 1980s when one of the prime gang violence prevention strategies was Operation Hammer (Google it). When I read about Jeff's work, I knew I had to meet him; I couldn't not. Jeff and I talked about his work and its inception. In 2007, he and his gang violence prevention team had to start somewhere, so they picked the "obvious"—the middle of the night in the most violent parks in the city, working with young people at risk of joining a gang or already involved in one.

Working with many others in the community, he helped develop a program called "Summer Night Lights," which kept parks open through the night with organized activities. Jeff used his experience with other programs but felt there might be a better way to combine multiple tactics. In 2008, they started in eight parks. Jeff recruited at-risk youths who had already joined gangs to manage the parks and told them, "You are here because you were *chosen*." He was giving these young people the opportunity to change their life narrative from one of villain to hero. Jeff firmly believed that if you changed gang members' self-perception, you could eventually change their behavior and their lives.

Jeff explained what it felt like. "At first, it was pretty hard; many of the people who had been my friends and colleagues at other community-based organizations seemed to turn against me when I took the city money they had relied upon and created a new strategy and new focus. It meant that some folks couldn't continue the work they were doing. While this was hard, I knew I had to stay the course and follow through with the change, or we would never get the results we needed. We had a window of opportunity and our job was to get as much done as quickly as we could so that we could keep that window propped open as long as possible and drive as much change through it as we could before it closed." In this work, you face choices like which matters more, keeping friends or helping the kids in our communities that need us to stand up for them? If you decide to take it on, this work won't be easy, but it can be life-changing; and that's a trade-off worth making.

That first summer, the number of homicides in Los Angeles parks went from eight in 2007 to zero in 2008. Overall gang crime dropped 20 percent. The next summer, the program grew to 16 parks, then 24, then 32, with at-risk young people filling more key leadership roles. They were achieving what others felt was impossible.

In 2012, Los Angeles had fewer total homicides (299) citywide than it had gang homicides alone in 2002 (350) and in 1992 (430). Between 2003 and 2013, gang-related robberies in the city fell from 3,274 to 1,021; gang assaults from 3,063 to 1,611. And in 2014, the Los Angeles Police Department announced that gang crime had dropped by nearly half since 2008.[3] Need more data to prove we do not lack solutions? Jeff Carr would never consider himself a superhero. Andy Lipkis and Suzi Levine wouldn't either. Like the regular heroes they are, they were just doing something they couldn't not do.

Seven Questions That Unleash Potential

Maybe you, or someone you know, are a little like Andy, Suzi, Jeff, or Bill. You have that internal feeling that you want to do more for your community, to find and give more to that cause that you can't not do something about. As you read this book, meet the characters, and read the stories, I hope you will also engage in an internal dialogue with seven underlying questions. These seven simple questions get at the heart of why certain people reach their greatest potential for social change:

1. Are you a determined optimist?
2. Who are you at your core?
3. Are you willing to go to hard places?
4. Are you ready to be humble *and* humbled?
5. Can you *actively* listen?
6. Do you believe 1 + 1 = 3?
7. What is your can't not do?

Using this book, you can work through answering these questions one at a time, thinking through them in order or jump around. Maybe a few of them speak to you more now than others, so start there. You definitely don't need to answer them all at once. It's not like the people you'll read about in these pages ever sat down and took a seven-question quiz; I sort of reverse-engineered and simplified what I learned over 17 years. These questions are most surely the ones they commonly faced, wrestled with and are living out. Answering them will give you a road map to finding your can't not do.

What matters, then, is that you really chew on at least one or two of these to get you started, allowing the question to stick in your mind and open new possibilities to how you see yourself and your choices in life. Open your mind to impulses that may be inside you, waiting to be released. In short, start to unlock your potential to transform your world and the way you serve others.

Why ask questions instead of give answers? The first boss I had out of college, when I was bright-eyed and full of energy and optimism, drove me crazy. When I went to him for answers, he'd ask questions. When I proposed an answer or solution to a particular problem, he'd have more questions. It drove me nuts, and I wondered what was wrong with this guy and how he'd ever gotten a job there in the first place.

Ten years later, he rose to be the CEO—for all the right reasons— of that Fortune 500 company, and I've long since learned the power of the right question. One great question is far more powerful than a dozen answers. A question asks people to think through the problem and own the answer for themselves, far more deeply and powerfully than just giving them the answer ever would. It took me a while, but I came to recognize that my boss's frustrating questions were actually a great gift. Thanks, Brad.

I know that it takes more than just a question to make change happen. But I also know the people who dare to open their hearts to ask themselves and authentically answer these questions are the ones who will take big steps and truly create big changes in our future.

The Undeniable Question

One of the wonderful things about writing a book like this is that many of the people you will read about helped me create it, mainly by how they live their lives. They also gave me feedback, ideas, input, and made it far better than I could have on my own. One of those people is Larry Fox, a financial guy from Portland, Oregon. Those financial types are usually sort of linear, literal thinkers, ya know. Not Larry. He is one of the deepest thinkers I've ever met; every time I'd show him a piece of this book, he'd come back with a way to improve it. Thanks, Larry.

In one of his notes he said to me, "I want to know what *the undeniable question* is that inspires me and is unsettling enough for me to change my otherwise less-motivated self. And not just move myself into predisposed paths, which is just fulfillment of who I am today. I want fulfillment of who I am *not*—not now, but potentially able to be. Something like, what would you be if you could be the person that God, or the person you value most, wants you to be?" Another way of asking what's your can't not do?

A Little about SVP and Me

My roots start in the Midwest; I grew up in Iowa. My dad was a minister and my mom was a mom's mom. I was the baby of the family and I got married a little too early to the right, and I mean *right*, girl. I got my MBA in Texas, was a product manager at Nestlé, spent time in and loved Los Angeles, launched a start-up in Boston that did not make it (bad idea with a three-month-old baby in tow), and rounded things off with a stop at Microsoft for six years in the 1990s. I have three sons who make me proud, damn proud. And, for the past 17 years, I have been with Social Venture Partners (SVP).

Many, though definitely not all, of the people I talk about in this book are regular heroes I have met at my not-so-regular place of work. In 1998, I was given a job that was, and is, so much more than just a job. SVP wasn't my idea to begin with, so I'm free to talk about how great the founders' concept was without any hesitation. I've been a steward for the vision of Paul Brainerd, Scott Oki, Maggie and Doug Walker, Bill Neukom, and Ida Cole. They created SVP and have enabled thousands of people all over the globe to find what they can't not do.

SVP builds powerful relationships between people who want to give back and the nonprofits and social entrepreneurs that make change possible. We help people build their civic and philanthropic potential through peer grant making and networking and help nonprofits build stronger organizations though strategic volunteering and collaboration. A quick note here about the word "nonprofit"—I'll use it throughout the book to refer to organizations focused on positive social change; in today's world, that might be a nonprofit or a for-profit social enterprise, or a public benefit corporation. Consider those terms interchangeable; it's great that we have more diverse organizations cropping up!

SVP's vision? We envision a community in which, regardless of income, class, or race, all children receive an excellent education and all people live and work in a healthy environment. Our mission? SVP cultivates effective philanthropists and strengthens organizations driving community change, building powerful relationships that advance shared community goals.

It's all about engagement and connection. The magic, if you will, is in putting all these parts together. It's not just one of the parts—the grant making, the volunteering, the networking—because you can find each of them standalone somewhere in your community. It's all of it mixed together. It's how SVP makes $1 + 1 + 1 = 10$. It is how so many people find they have more to give because they give alongside others. And it's the power and leverage of a network, brought to bear to help solve social problems and catalyze the future civic and philanthropic leaders of our community, all at the same time.

The founders' original vision in 1997 fit the dot-com, new-wealth, be-more-engaged ethos of those times. The timing for this current, international model of SVP in our hyperconnected, hands-on, socially responsible world of 2015 is even better. It is out of SVP that many of these stories grow, but their messages extend far beyond. Do you need to be in SVP to create impact? Most definitely not.

How to Use This Book

- Introduction and the Multipliers. These will orient you to the title of this book and why your can't not do matters now more than ever.
- Part I, Chapters 1–3—Finding Your Focus, contains three questions that will help you define your can't not do. These will help you lay down your foundation, get clarity, and understand what your "true north" is.
- Part II, Chapters 4–6—How You Do This Work Well, offers three more questions designed to help you put your can't not do into action. Once you've defined your can't not do, how do you best show up in your community to be most effective and help others around you create more positive impact, too?
- Part III, Chapters 7 and 8 and the Conclusion—Bringing It All Together for Your World and You. This section brings everything full circle with the ultimate question and also offers a few different ways to embed your answers in your mind and heart.
- Appendices. Resources here will help you answer questions like, what's the checklist to help me intentionally work this through for myself? Which stories in this book are most relevant to me? What other resources are out there for me? And more.

You can dive in just about anywhere in the book, just get started, but keep in mind how the chapters interconnect. I hope you might read the three parts in order, but for the three chapters within each part, I think you can jump around. Each chapter concludes with five key ideas, but I hope you'll make lots of notes in the margins with your own important ideas, as you read along. The appendices at the end will give you more ideas and tips to effectively put all of these ideas into motion in your community. And if you don't get enough in the pages of this book, go to www.paulshoemaker.org/.

And let me say a little more about *who* this book is (and isn't) for.

- It doesn't matter if your politics are left or right, the ideas in this book don't tilt either way.
- These ideas are not faith- or religion-dependent. Depending on your faith, you may or may not see a lot of resonant ideas, but whatever your religion, this book isn't driven by any specific faith.
- It's not a specific, narrowly defined book about how to start a nonprofit or be a social entrepreneur or a great philanthropist, although I've included a few of those kinds of books in the Appendix. This is about people, regular heroes who want to make a positive impact on the world, whatever walk of life they come from.
- And if some of the people here seem like they've done more than you possibly could at this point in your life, and maybe that's true, please do *not* assume you can't learn any lessons from them. None of us are Martin Luther King, Jr. or Rosa Parks, but we often glean life lessons from heroes like them; you can do the same here.

In general, the concepts here are most (though not only) resonant with people at transition points in life, people who have had a significant positive or negative event happen recently and who have some predisposition to create meaningful positive change in the world. If you are a person who has met a lot of basic needs in life and has already realized some level of success, acclaim, or achievement, you probably have the right frame of mind that will enable you to get the most out of the seven questions. In the end, the person who will know best if this book is for you is . . . you! I hope you're ready to find your can't not do!

■ ■ ■

Our world's social challenges—education, poverty, leadership development, urban ecosystems, homelessness, and so on—aren't getting easier. But the opportunity and the potential to create significant, positive change has never been greater. It's a race between opposing forces and our communities hang in the balance. On the one hand, are the complexity of our social challenges and the speed at which our world changes and on the other, the collective know-how and human and financial resources we can bring to bear on them. Can't-not-do people are the ones who will help decide who wins that race.

So what's *your* can't not do? To me, this is *the* fundamental question. This book will have served its purpose if the personal stories and questions inspire more people to ask this of themselves and to get on board with taking deeper, longer-term, effective action. As I was doing my last edits on this manuscript, Bill and Melinda Gates penned their annual letter on their "Big Bets for the Future."[4] They talked about specific progress they foresaw in impoverished parts of the world, but they also emphasized that "we think there has never been a better time to accelerate progress and have a big impact around the world."

And they didn't just mean themselves. They went on to say, "There's a crucial factor: informed, passionate individuals working together to form effective movements for change . . . . We call them global citizens [I call them can't-not-do people] . . . . The more global citizens (www.globalcitizen.org) there are, and the more active and effective they are, the more progress we will make . . . . In fact, we're betting on it." I'll double down on that bet with Bill and Melinda right now.

In closing, the morning of August 9, 2013, and the loss of Bill was a jolt. I hate everything about that day. It still shakes me to my core when I think about it. But it spurred me to quit waiting any longer to share what I have learned with people like you. The only time I could find to write this book was between the hours of 3:00 A.M. and 6:00 A.M. every other morning for about three months. But I absolutely had to write it; yes, I couldn't not. I hope you won't wait any longer to take the next step, be it small or big, on your path to unlocking your potential to help change our world.

Margaret Mead famously said, "Never doubt a small group of committed citizens can change the world; indeed, it's the only thing that ever has." On those inspiring words I'd put a twist, because I've witnessed it again and again and again: "Never doubt the power of *one* committed citizen to *start to* change the world." That one can be you.

Five Key Ideas from the Prologue

1. Your can't not do might be about a particular social issue like K–12 education or homelessness, or it might be some personal expertise or passion like leadership development, community engagement, and so on.
2. Don't try to tackle all seven questions at once. Start with one or two that resonate most and then, over time, dig deeper into the other questions so someday you've dealt with all of them.
3. This book isn't for famous people or only for people with lots of money; it's about what each of us can do, as regular heroes, in our neighborhoods and our world.
4. For some people, this will become a full-time endeavor, and for others it will be part-time or a few hours a week. You'll find stories of people all over that spectrum in this book.
5. If you will dig deeply and purposefully into these seven questions, you *will* find your pathway to creating more impact in your world and a more purposeful, meaningful life.

INTRODUCTION: WHY OUR SOCIAL DRIVES MATTER MORE NOW—MULTIPLIERS

Continuous effort—not strength or intelligence—is the key to unlocking our potential.

—Winston Churchill

On February 21, 2003, Liu Jianlun, a Chinese doctor, attended a wedding in Hong Kong, during which he stayed at the Metropole Hotel in room 911. Within 24 hours, he was admitted to an intensive care unit. On the following day, a Chinese-American businessman, Johnny Chen, who had stayed at the Metropole across the hall from Liu, traveled on to Hanoi, Vietnam. He became ill and was admitted to the French Hospital of Hanoi where he was treated by Dr. Carlo Urbani. Jianlun died on March 4. Chen died on March 13. And Dr. Urbani died on March 29. Chen was patient zero for the SARS pandemic.[1]

Severe Acute Respiratory Syndrome, or SARS, originated with a farmer in the Guangdong province of China, and its worldwide spread was set in motion in a matter of a few days on the ninth floor of that hotel in Hong Kong. SARS is a very serious form of pneumonia, which can lead to acute respiratory distress, severe breathing difficulty, and sometimes death. If you're like me, you hear that phrase, scratch your head and eventually think, *Oh yeah, that virus from about 10 years ago!* SARS broke out in 2003, and the word "pandemic" suddenly became part of our collective vocabulary. SARS quickly spread across the globe. I remember feeling a growing anxiety as each day passed and the headlines of doom screamed louder and louder.

Dr. Urbani, unlike other doctors at the hospital who thought Chen had a bad case of influenza, realized that Chen was potentially infected with something more like a highly contagious disease. Tragically, Dr. Urbani was also infected and died a month later. A Chinese doctor, a Chinese-American, a hotel in Hong Kong, a plane flight to Vietnam and a trip to see an Italian doctor at the French Hospital—the *perils* of globalization, all in a matter of days.

Before he became ill, Urbani notified the World Health Organization (WHO) and became one of those regular heroes by triggering the most effective response to a major epidemic in history. The WHO subsequently set up 11 research labs worldwide in an unprecedented massive collaboration. Each pursued its own lines of investigation but shared data real time, conferencing daily over the phone and web. Just a week after the project began, the team of labs isolated a candidate virus. Within a month, the labs deciphered the virus' genetic code to unmask its true identity: SARS. Four months after the first outbreak outside of China, the epidemic was contained, due to unmatched international collaboration—the *promise* of globalization, all in a matter of days.

The global crisis started with one person, Johnny Chen, and the solution to this global challenge began with another person, Dr. Carlo Urbani. A news story at the time of his death related that Dr. Urbani had an argument with his wife. She said it wasn't responsible behavior for the father of three children to risk his life treating such sick patients. Dr. Urbani replied, "If I can't work in such situations, what am I here for? Answering e-mails, going to cocktail parties, and pushing paper?"

We Face a Pivotal Moment, a Tipping Point of Multipliers

We know the pace of change and forces at play in the world—globalization, connectedness, technology—are accelerating. That's not new news. We can learn, share, and connect faster than ever before. That's what happened with the SARS outbreak. Ultimately, it was one of the shining examples of the promise of our global, connected world. Inherent within those changes are also perils; we need look no further than 9/11 to see the worst of it. Or imagine what would have happened if Dr. Urbani and the WHO hadn't put aside jurisdictions and egos to respond to SARS with such impassioned collaboration and connectedness.

More than ever before, in the past 10 to 20 years, just a *few* people can do *so* much. These advances in globalization, connectedness, and technology are converging to become *force multipliers* that can either increase the magnitude of social problems or accelerate the solutions to them. The concept of force multipliers originated in the military and refers to a combination of attributes that make a given force more effective than that same force would be without those attributes.[2] A simple example is a hammer; it amplifies or multiplies the force of swinging your arm.

In more general use, a force multiplier refers to a factor that dramatically increases, hence multiplies, the effectiveness of an item or group. People like Andy, Suzi, or Dr. Urbani can now do so much more because of globalization, connectedness, and technology. We live in a world where the impact one person can have is multiplied far more greatly than it ever has been before. That's a pretty exciting reason for determined optimism.

From my work full-time all around social challenges, I can feel the power of those multipliers further accelerating in just the last five years. I have never been more excited (or worried), because these forces for social progress (or decline) are at an historic tipping point. With a growing sense of urgency, we need more committed people to find their can't not do to become the difference-makers, driving and putting those multipliers to work for change and tipping the balance toward a better world.

The Connected Passion of Anne Reece, Multiplied

Substantive positive change in public education seems almost impossible these days, probably the way gang violence in Los Angeles felt about 10 years ago. Don't tell that to Anne Reece, PhD, the third-year principal at White Center Heights Elementary School. Much like Jeff Carr in Los Angeles, I couldn't not meet Reece. The problem was, and is, she's always on the move, almost impossible to nail down to a sit-down. When I finally got ahold of her, the energy and passion came bursting across my phone; I almost needed to hold the receiver a few inches from my ear while I adjusted to her volume.

An Aussie, she studied at the Ontario Institute for Education and found her way to her first elementary teaching job in a Seattle suburb. She was "astounded by the glaring disparities" she saw for young kids in the United States; she wasn't used to that from her life experiences in Australia and Canada. Reece told me she believes our school system has "let some kids down instead of lifting them up." She knew working in one classroom wasn't going to be enough. So after two years in the classroom, a doctoral program, and one year as an assistant principal, the Highline School District brought on a new principal, born halfway around the world, to lead one of the most challenged schools in greater Seattle.

She remembers feeling on her first day, "Holy sh—, this is going to be a lot of work." On the job only six days in 2012, Reece took her staff through a thorough, at times very hard, review of student test results, trying to get at what had worked . . . or had not. "I kind of blasted them out of the water, I'll admit," she said. Yet after that early meeting, teachers applauded and one sent a note afterward: "Enjoyed the take-charge stance. Stay strong."[3]

When Reece took the helm, 60 to 70 percent of her third-, fourth-, fifth-, and sixth-graders could not read at grade level. "The potential of these kids was way higher than the data showed, I could see that immediately," she said. "But our teachers had lost so much hope that they weren't even focusing on academics anymore. These were smart, capable people, but they'd lost faith in their ability to teach."[4]

When Reece tells White Center Heights' story, she refers to "my kids," "my teachers," and "my community." Her sense of passion and caring are bountiful. She has "totally bought into these students" and wants to stay at the school to "see it all the way through." The longer I talked to her that day, the more I liked her, the more energized I was, the more I believed in the power of one person, multiplied by all of those teachers, parents and, of course, students!

Instead of drilling students with exercises and worksheets, teachers began challenging them to reflect on the meaning of stories rather than simply remembering and reciting words. Reece paid teachers to study instructional theory on their own time, giving them time to meet in groups and discuss their findings. Success required teachers to constantly reevaluate their students.[5]

Reece has her 27 teachers organized into an array of vertical and horizontal teams (her terminology). The self-selected vertical teams focus on math, reading, English, and so on, and the horizontal ones are oriented by grade and academic levels. She doesn't need a lot of new, additional technology, and this isn't going global, but she is creating a myriad of new, stronger connections all across that school and community. The wisdom and knowledge are there to be tapped, if only we will connect it. They didn't need new solutions (they already had them) or more money (that wasn't the main barrier); they needed one regular hero to lead and 27 who were ready to get on board.

With a minimal increase in funding and no change in teachers, the school achieved a seemingly impossible jump in student achievement in one year, in every grade—all rising by double-digit percentiles. District leaders even worried about cheating for a brief time, but

White Center Heights Elementary, with 88 percent of kids on free or reduced-price lunch, showed some of the biggest gains for math and reading in the entire state.

This is a story of what works. We know how to teach our kids, contrary to what much of society believes. It takes smart, good people, connected to each other, their students, and their community, bringing together their knowledge and wisdom and shared effort. District Superintendent Susan Enfield explained, "This is not about some whiz-bang curriculum." There is a triumvirate of school staff, committed parents, and high-potential students that multiplies into results and better lives than would have ever been possible individually.

There is not just the empirical evidence at White Center Heights, but research-based evidence from the Carnegie Foundation for the Advancement of Teaching, where they spent 10 years examining the changing quality of "relational dynamics," that is, the health of relationships between the organizations and individuals in the school system, in 400 Chicago elementary schools.[6] Their work led to a metric called "relational trust" to categorize the social exchanges among students, teachers, parents, and principals, as exemplified by Dr. Reece and the White Center Heights community. Their main conclusion: the level of relational trust, another way of framing connectedness, was a more powerful discriminator between improving and nonimproving schools than curriculum design, teaching practices, or socioeconomic factors.

This kind of powerful, good work happens every day in individual classrooms all over the United States, just not in enough of them yet. The price tag for the adjustments at White Center Heights was nominal, about $75,000 incrementally, in total; that's a few hundred dollars per student per year. No one is declaring victory, but after failing to gain traction for years, teachers achieved something that eludes educators across the country: they jump-started a turnaround, and they did it in just nine months. Nine months. Perhaps most notable is that they achieved this without any big staff turnover or by sending weaker students off to other schools. They focused on improved instruction and collaboration.

The momentum driving academic achievement has continued in Reece's second and third years at the school. At last fall's kickoff meeting with teachers, Reece told them simply, "The reality is, we can be kind to them, we can love them. It doesn't break the cycle of poverty. Education is the only way."

We've Seen This Movie in a Different Town

Today's rapid acceleration of globalization, connectedness, and technology is not a new story. We are used to seeing those intertwined forces applied aggressively and successfully as multipliers to private sector business:

- For many years, the trend was to outsource car-making to Asian countries. In more recent years, Asian car companies are increasingly manufacturing their cars in the United States. A car is a global amalgamation of parts and pieces. When I visit other parts of the world, I am acutely aware of the differences in culture, but globalization has also given us so many more ways to find commonality.
- It seems commonplace today, but traveling with my smartphone, I can text, search the Internet, and make calls just as easily to someone halfway around the world as to my next door neighbor. The sense of connectedness created is as profound as it is seemingly simple.
- Facebook and its underlying technology barely existed 10 years ago; today it reaches nearly 20 percent of the world's population. And via that medium, messages today can spread globally in no time, whether they be a cry for help or a racist comment or another celebratory post about how well someone's child is now doing in school. The technology of Twitter flips the logic of connectedness on its head. It's faster than CNN; news departments today get their

updates from Twitter, not the other way around. For example, a remarkable series of tweets over the course of several hours revealed the death of Osama bin Laden at the hands of U.S. Navy SEALs before any news network, and with such speed that it may have forced a statement from President Obama sooner than his staff may have preferred.[7]

But, while we have aggressively applied these three multipliers in the private sector for the past 10 to 20 years to solve consumer and business-related problems, we have barely scratched the surface of applying these same multipliers to solving social problems, whether through nonprofit or private sector means. Think about how drastically our commerce, products, and services have changed in 20 years. Now think about what positive social change is possible in the next 20 years when we bring those same multipliers to bear much more aggressively than we have to date in solving our most intractable social challenges. It's time, and we will.

The SARS success story showed one way of leveraging the multiplier of globalization for a social cause. Reece and White Center Heights is an example of leveraging the multiplier of connectedness. Jack Maple is a success story about technology.

How Pins Stuck in a Map on the Wall Can Reduce Crime

Jack Maple was born in 1952 and grew up in Richmond Hill, New York, right between Queens and John F. Kennedy International Airport. He was a classic New Yorker and lived there his whole life. As a teenager, he worked odd jobs while earning his equivalency diploma from Brooklyn Tech High at night. Maple went on to become a transit police officer, patrolling the city's subways.[8] It was one of the most dangerous jobs in New York City.

To help reduce the crime he was encountering, Maple came up with a seemingly simple plan: track robberies in the subways, which represented the majority of violent crime on his beat, by pinpointing their locations with pins stuck in maps on his wall. It was originally called Charts of the Future and is credited with cutting subway crime significantly, because he could dispatch officers to hot spots, accordingly. In the 1980s, Maple used maps, several hundred of them, on walls in the offices of his precinct, to identify those patterns. Sort of like *A Beautiful Mind*[9] for crime-solvers.

William J. Bratton was the Chief of New York City Transit Police at the time. When he was appointed Police Commissioner for New York City in 1994, he brought Maples and his Charts with him. Eventually Bratton got the NYPD to adopt the system, which Maple renamed CompStat (computer analysis of statistics). By then, the system had evolved from pins stuck in maps on walls. They used computerized maps to pinpoint where crime was taking place and ran computer analysis instead of relying on visual recognition of crime patterns. In 1994, the year CompStat was adopted, murders in New York City dropped from 1,946 to 1,561, with another dramatic decline in 1995 to 1,177.[10] The rates continued a downward trajectory and by 2005 had reached levels below those of the early 1960s. In 2014, the number had dropped to 328. While the decline cannot be solely attributed to CompStat, most crime researchers and officials believe the program was a major factor.

Similar systems were adopted by other police forces across the United States. In part because of good ideas married with technology like CompStat and people like Maple, policing has become more effective over the past two decades and violent crime in the United States has declined by nearly half. *Violent crime has declined by nearly half.* Are we all aware of that, given the often-contradictory headlines and media hype we see all the time?

Today, CompStat is a fairly well-known success story. It represents one of the most obvious, explicit uses of technology to change the trajectory of a social challenge in the United States. It was pioneered by one regular hero, Jack Maple, who, rather than just walking his beat and accepting things the way they were, saw something he couldn't not do. His idea was adopted and scaled up by William Bratton, who has become something of a superhero in the world of policing. The application of technology to a social problem doesn't often have such a straight line connecting intervention and result, but CompStat won't be the last time technology is brought to bear in a new and profound way to address big social challenges in the next 20 years.

The Bottom Line

As we move toward the future, the one element that is most needed to bring these three social multipliers together in profoundly new ways are more people like Carlo Urbani, Anne Reece, and Jack Maple and others—potentially you—who are finding and pursuing their can't not do. Now more than ever, a few people, even one person, can have huge positive impact. The forces of good and evil are fighting their age-old battle but with new and better tools. The difference maker, the main catalyst that turns those multipliers into forces for good, is can't-not-do people, like each of you.

In-the-trenches, battle-tested experience tells us that more people today have the right stuff for this work than we, or even they, think. To change the world does not require superhuman abilities, special destinies, or even a life-consuming commitment. It requires something more attainable: the intentional combination of a personal urge to make a difference with deep, deliberate, self-reflection and action on a few key questions, seven to be exact.

I'll share what I've learned, woven through a narrative of real-life stories, from my 17 years of daily, real-time interaction with successful, determined difference makers. Together, this catalyzing mix unlocks people's potential, their can't-not-do that has proven, again and again, to be the compelling social drive that can change our world.

Five Key Ideas from the Introduction

1. Globalization, connectedness, and technology have accelerated the impact one person can have, more than ever before.
2. Those three multipliers have had their greatest impact in the private sector, but their effects, over the next 10 to 20 years, will be felt just as powerfully in the social sector.
3. Can't-not-do people are the most effective catalysts that use those multipliers to create greater social impact.
4. We are near a tipping point on many social challenges in the next generation, and can't-not-do people will tip that balance.
5. To help change the world does not require superhuman abilities, special destinies, or even a life-consuming commitment. It does take determined, intentional focus.

PART I

Finding Your Focus

CHAPTER 1

David Risher, the Lost Key, and Eradicating Illiteracy

Are You a Determined Optimist?

Don't ask what the world needs. Ask what makes you come alive, and go do it. Because what the world needs is people who have come alive.

—Howard Thurman

"I knew at a very young age I was a reader. My mom instilled the belief in me that 'if I don't have reading, I have nothing.'" When David Risher was five, his parents divorced, leaving his mom to support the family. Those were not easy times growing up. Mom didn't have much work experience, but did find a job selling encyclopedias. The money was just enough, at times barely, to support the family and, just as important to her, filled their house with encyclopedias.

David will tell you he has been a reader for as long as he can remember. So for a kid like David who loved to read, his mom's job was the perfect setup. Books on any subject were literally everywhere. When his mom ran errands, she would drop the boys off at the library. When he walked to school, it was always with a book in his hand. He was passionate about books. Reading is part of David's core self.

He was one of the first people I got to know in my new job back in 1991. I definitely didn't think "superhero" when I met him. He seemed like a regular Joe. He was a soft-spoken, never-full-of-himself kind of human being. There was a quiet confidence and a sort of sparkle in the guy's eyes. Still is.

When you sit down with him, he has this disarmingly casual, friendly, laid-back way about him. You quickly feel comfortable. Then David starts talking fast, really fast. So fast that sometimes you struggle to keep up. But you always feel like his words and ideas come from a place of authenticity and purposefulness. He's not just spouting stuff off the top of his head. He's genuine; I don't think he has an insincere bone in his body. As I got to know him, it was easy to see this guy is passionate. He is passionate about technology and education, and especially about books.

A few years ago, David and his wife, Jen, and their two daughters went on a long-term working vacation. They taught school overseas, helped build a house in Vietnam, and ended up spending several weeks helping out at an orphanage in Ecuador. His young kids carried e-readers during their travels. The technology was just hitting the mass market, and his kids brought them along to keep up on their school work.

David's passions—books, education, and technology—came crashing together at that orphanage. Walking across the grounds on a hot summer morning, he noticed a padlocked building across from the school and wondered what was in the building that had to be kept under lock and key. "That's our library," explained the orphanage's leader. David asked to see what was inside the library, but the leader admitted, "I think we've lost the key."

At that moment, no one seemed overly concerned about the unused building, except David. He noticed his kids reading voraciously on their e-readers, just a short distance from the orphaned children. He looked at his kids with their devices. He looked at the orphanage children. He looked at the inaccessible library. Back at his kids. Back at the orphaned children and the padlock. As David puts it, "There were my own kids reading on these devices, while I'm looking at these other kids, with that same drive to learn, but without even basic tools." And David got an idea.

His mind was racing. He looked at a seemingly hopeless situation at a disadvantaged orphanage in a remote part of the world through a different lens from most others. He saw a real problem and thought he could have an answer. Most people would have seen the locked building and the bookless orphans and either failed to give them another thought or written the situation off as just another intractable social problem and walked away.

Instead, David had an aha moment: a simple and optimistic vision of bringing e-readers to parts of the world that needed them most. His mind was flooded with ideas. "I thought to myself, okay, hold on. I can step back and think, I'm going to just watch kids who are hungry to learn not have the books they need to improve their lives or I can step in and say, let's solve this problem." He stepped in, all the way in, during those moments in the courtyard, thousands of miles from home.

When David returned to the United States, he helped conceive and launch Worldreader (www.worldreader.org), a nonprofit that uses technology to bring reading material to areas most in need. He found a like-minded partner in Colin McElwee, and together they developed David's kernel of an idea into a working model: Combine the extensive availability of mobile technology, the falling costs of e-readers, and the power of letting children choose which books they want to read. Ultimately, lives throughout the world could be transformed.

David was starting a new business, just like he'd done before many times in his professional life. He was very good at seeing a new opportunity and putting the plans, people, resources, and next steps together; it was almost like muscle memory to him. He wrote an action plan, and with that, Worldreader was born.

Today, David believes widespread illiteracy can be eradicated in the most heavily afflicted parts of the developing world. That is his fundamental, determined optimism. It is his *one* thing, his *can't not do* in which he firmly believes. He may not have the answer to ending gang violence or early childhood development issues; he can leave those challenges to someone else. But David knows he can help end illiteracy someday.

Let's be clear: The challenge of illiteracy is not a small one. Over the past 100 years, rates of global illiteracy have dropped from 75 percent to less than 15 percent. But according to UNESCO, that means there are still 773.5 million illiterate people in this world and 123.2 million children of primary school age who lack basic reading and writing skills.[1] Extremely low literacy rates are focused in three regions: South Asia, West Asia, and Sub-Saharan Africa. Fifty percent of sub-Saharan schools have few or no books at all. David has done his research and knows this, but when presented with the prospect of putting an e-book into hands of an eager young reader, he has never equated daunting statistics with impossible.

"Once I came up with the idea," says David about starting Worldreader, "how could I *not?*"

When I first talked to David, Worldreader had an active presence in nine African countries, 27 worldwide through its Worldreader mobile app, and in its first four years since inception, nearly 1.8 million e-books had been read, and there were nearly 200,000 kids reading every quarter. It was real progress, but such a long journey to go, just the kind of challenge for a determined optimist. There's an update since I checked several months ago: as of March 2015, over 2.2 million e-books have been read, more than 400,000 kids in 50 countries are reading every quarter, and the rate is accelerating (check the home page at www.worldreader.org). And why would it not in this world of multipliers and determined optimists like David? What a great example of using technology as a social multiplier.

David is fundamentally optimistic about the kids around the world that he wants to help; it's what drives his can't-not-do spirit. When I first asked him about the kids Worldreader is working with, I expected to hear how bad things were, how long the odds were. The first words out of his mouth were about how "curious, hungry to learn, and enthusiastic" these kids are; David doesn't see needy, he sees potential. "Reading is our main vaccine against poverty," he says, echoing Anne Reece's belief about education and his own experience of reading as a way out of poverty while growing up.

What's the Point?

If you're going to dive into this change-the-world business, you better believe that solving the problem at hand is possible. Can we eradicate illiteracy in the developing world (and at home)? Can we develop more and more strong leaders for the social sector? Can we create a United States in which every child shows up on the first day of kindergarten with an equal opportunity to learn? Can we dramatically reduce gang violence in our major urban areas? If a particular social problem was an easy one to solve, it's probably already been solved; so the ones that are left can feel impossible to a lot of, sometimes most, people. But not to everyone.

Like David Risher, determined optimists are people who believe a solution to a given social problem is possible. I don't use the term *determined optimist* in some airy-fairy sense. I'm talking about hardcore problem solvers who do not believe "no" is a viable answer.

I'm about 65 percent determination and 35 percent optimism; everyone is different. If I had to guess, I'd say David is the opposite from me; that's just a gut feel, it's what he exudes. I wouldn't say I'm pessimistic, but I'm also not a naturally optimistic person, though I wish I were. I'm more of a realist who believes change is possible; there is a reason Teddy Roosevelt's "man in the arena" quote (pardon the gender skew) is my favorite of all time. I'm more of a grinder; when I get focused, I get determined, really determined, but at the end of the day you also have to have belief, enough optimism to know that change is possible, like David.

> *It is not the critic who counts; not the man who points out how the strong man stumbles, or where the doer of deeds could have done them better. The credit belongs to the man who is actually in the arena, whose face is marred by dust and sweat and blood; who strives valiantly; who errs, who comes short again and again, because there is no effort without error and shortcoming; but who does actually strive to do the deeds; who knows great enthusiasms, the great devotions; who spends himself in a worthy cause; who at the best knows in the end the triumph of high achievement, and who at the worst, if he fails, at least fails while daring greatly, so that his place shall never be with those cold and timid souls who neither know victory nor defeat.*
>
> — Teddy Roosevelt

Determined optimists see their chosen social challenge as a puzzle to be solved, not a hopelessly entrenched problem. Being a determined optimist about a single cause or area of focus is a key principle here. The world changes when enough people get focused and go deep on one challenge; cue the Margaret Mead quote again about committed people, also known as determined optimists. Note that I said "challenge," not "challenges." You don't need to feel determined optimism about many things. In fact, you only have to feel that optimistic about one thing in life. One cause. You can leave all the other problems to other people, people who are just as optimistic about impacting those problems. What's vital is that each of us finds that one cause and commits to it for the long term.

Think about gang violence in Los Angeles. I lived there from 1985 to 1990 with my wife, Lori. She taught at an inner city school, Hoover Street Elementary, the biggest one west of the Mississippi, with well over 50 languages spoken. Ninety percent of the school's families at that time came to the United States to escape war and poverty in Central America. They were some of the most inspiring kids and families you'd ever want to meet. It was also in a neighborhood surrounded by dangerous gangs, including the Bloods and the Crips.

Gang violence permeated the news. At that time, nothing felt more intractable than gangs in L.A. And yet, as we've discussed, someone like Jeff Carr, not a superhero or a famous celebrity, viewed it as a complex human puzzle to solve. How do you reconfigure the people and conditions so the equation for gang violence sums up differently? Could it be done? Jeff and a handful of other determined optimists thought so. As we saw, they proved they were right. There's still a whole lot of work left to do, but the progress is amazing.

Optimism is a necessity for can't-not-do work because of its exceptional power to spur action, inspire others, and most important, provide the fuel to burn when the challenges seem greatest and determination is needed most. Determination and optimism fuel and reinforce each other. Daniel Kainer can shed some light on why. Dr. Kainer is the director of the Lone Star College Bio-technology Institute. He has written and spoken on a number of topics, and at a TEDx talk he spoke about the Power of Optimism.[2] A few of his findings are very relevant to our understanding of what determined optimism is and how it works:

- *Reality-based optimism trumps blind hope.* Optimism based on blind hope or wishful thinking can be downright dangerous. The kind of optimism we are talking about here is based on reality, what one can honestly control and not control. There is an "eyes on the prize" determination about these people. They are able to maintain their belief in the endgame, while knowing that solving these problems brings enormous complexity and constant change. This kind of determined optimism has real power and can help get you through the tough times and inevitable failures and roadblocks.

- *Persistent optimism is highly contagious.* Genuine, reality-based optimism breeds more optimism. And as one well-known social rule says, like attracts like. Change agents understand that you have to get others fired up about a cause, inspiring that same optimism in them and then building a team that can carry that optimism further. (Also see "Can you Actively Listen?" and "Do You Believe 1 + 1 = 3?" in later chapters.)

- *The right kind of optimism understands that the past is gone, but the future isn't here yet.* In other words, whatever conditions existed previously that resulted in an intractable problem (for example, smallpox outbreaks) have nothing to do with what can happen in the future (smallpox eradication). Determined optimists have a fundamental hopefulness and positivity. They look at a complex and entrenched problem and think, "This is hard, but a solution can be found." This kind of determined optimism is grounded in today's reality while looking to the horizon with a great sense of possibility.

Real change never happens because of just one person. It does take a community, a village, a whole school. There is absolutely no way the Davids, Suzis, Jeffs and other determined optimists of this world can make substantial change on their own. Nevertheless, you will almost always find one brave, determined, some might say irrational, optimist who got things started. Almost by definition, some *one* has to. One person's optimism is necessary though, ultimately, not sufficient. But it is, undoubtedly, the first domino in so many cases of positive social change.

Haven't Had That "Aha" Moment?

Does every successful change agent have an aha moment, like David Risher did? Some do, but many of us go optimistically toward a cause because we learn so much about a problem over time that we come to believe it is solvable. Eric Stowe is a perfect example.

Eric was a wanderer after he graduated from high school in the early 1990s. He'll be the first to tell you he didn't have a lot of direction, like lots of kids that age, and his wandering got him into some trouble a few times along the way. For six or seven years, he travelled around the United States working various odd jobs. Eventually he went to college and did research work for a professor on the history of U.S. civil rights. He and his girlfriend, now wife, still had that wanderlust in them so they traveled to China and Russia as part of their studies. During their time there, Eric began to see an intersection between what he was studying back home, the U.S. civil rights movement, and what he was seeing abroad in the developing social justice movements of Asia. "When I got back, I called my advisor, changed my major, and ended up doing the rest of my undergrad and my graduate degree, focusing on social justice movements," Eric explained.

He related all this to me over a few cups of coffee at one of those classic Seattle coffee houses on Capitol Hill. He seems perpetually young, not just because of his baby-face looks but because of the energy he brings to his work. He's also relentlessly open to feedback; he always wants to get better at what he does and improve as a better person. This openness isn't specific to one of the seven questions, but it's a trait I see and feel frequently from can't-not-do people.

In early 2003, as Eric was finishing up his degree, he got a call from someone who ran an international adoption agency and had heard that Eric had solid Chinese language skills. The man needed short-term help with 14 families going through Chinese adoptions. "It was like a busload of people and I shepherded them through their entire adoption process and I fell in love. Actually fell in love with the work," said Eric. He turned down a lucrative Washington, D.C., job offer, thinking to himself, "I have to figure out how to make this adoption agency guy give me a job." Then he spent the next three months convincing the man that he should. When he capitulated, Eric was hired and spent almost five years arranging international adoptions for abandoned and orphaned children, primarily from China, Vietnam, and Nepal. He interacted with several hundred orphanages across the globe. Eric was successful, but he couldn't help repeatedly asking himself, "In addition to finding homes for these children, what can I do for the kids still in those institutions? What can I do that will *last?*"

Eric made inquiries, conducted audits, and fielded questionnaires to many orphanage staff, searching for what would have the greatest impact. He eventually found his answer. Although the needs were innumerable, "it boiled down," said Eric, "to two defining things: better training for the caregivers and clean water." And for Eric, clean water seemed a no-brainer.

Providing safe and clean drinking water meets a fundamental need. In fact, the United Nations considers access to clean water a basic human right. Yet, nearly a billion people worldwide have limited access to clean water. The orphanages Eric saw certainly lacked it. But he also noticed that many orphanages coexisted in the same cities with U.S. fast-food chains that had no trouble finding a continual supply of clean water for their customers.

There is something else to know about Eric: he is tenacious and creative. He snuck into the kitchen at a McDonald's in China and wrote down the name of the manufacturer and the serial number for the water filtration system. If fast-food restaurants could provide clean water nearly anywhere in the world, he wanted to know why the same systems couldn't be used in places where children really needed them. Sounds a lot like David Risher and his experience with the e-readers and the locked library at the orphanage. "That juxtaposition seemed so easy to remediate—and it was," Eric explained.

With his employer's support, he spent a couple years contacting manufacturers of water purification equipment and getting relationships started, while raising money to install the systems at orphanages in China, Nepal, Vietnam, and Cambodia. His initiative was responsible for about 60 clean water projects at orphanages in 15 provinces in China alone. But even with this success, Eric was frustrated. "I was putting systems in, but I wasn't allowed to find out how the systems were functioning over time."

In August 2006 on a business trip to Cambodia, "over a huge beer and just pissed off," Eric wrote a 10-page manifesto detailing how one could scale his process of using water filtration systems to provide children with clean water, make the model sustainable, and build out a business for it. With this, Eric created the nonprofit A Child's Right, today renamed Splash.org, to provide water filtration systems that ensure safe water for children living at "the intersection of two streets: 'greatest degrees of poverty' and 'worst water quality conditions.'" Eric's optimism was contagious. When he returned to Seattle after laying his groundwork, he inspired a "guerilla-style cadre of volunteers who packed mountains of suitcases with pipes, filtration systems, and tools and set off for Kathmandu" and the like.[3]

To remind us how hard and messy this work can be, and there will be plenty of messes along the way (see Chapter 3, which focuses on hard places), Eric said he spent his first year getting his nonprofit off the ground as he continued his job in adoption, because he needed to pay rent. He worked his agency job during the day and ran the new organization at night. He describes that year as "the worst ever," but also as a catalytic year, a choice he never regrets. Just how "worst ever" did it get for him?

"Money, or lack thereof, was the first pause for me, but fear of failure undergirded those moments of hesitation at every step. Money just became an excuse to keep stalling. But honestly, the unknown didn't help either. I had a stable job, a lot of families that looked to my assistance in that role, working in international adoption, a young family of my own, a very young son with continuous health issues, and I traveled enough to be frustrating for all, but also exciting for me, adding a whole new endeavor—a start-up that no one else had done before, meaning no road map to plagiarize. That mix seemed unreasonable, untenable, impossible. And it was. That first year I worked both jobs; I doubled my travel duties, more than 200,000 miles in that year, and operated in at least eight different time zones day in and day out. I have, and this is no lie, almost fully repressed that year from memory. My wife and I both remember very little from it." I don't know about you, but I'm exhausted just *reading* about that year in Eric's life.

But Eric Stowe is the quintessential determined optimist and he forged on. His vision is "a world with clean water for all children and a museum telling of when it was not so." Can you get any more optimistic than having a museum for the problem you aim to eradicate in your vision statement? Can you sense how much determination it took, without which, all of the optimism in the world would have been squashed many times along his life journey already? In Eric's case, maybe determination alone isn't sufficient. Tenacity? Fearlessness? All of those.

Today Splash.org projects provide water and sanitation education to hundreds of thousands of children in Cambodia, China, Nepal, Vietnam, India, and Thailand. The amount of knowledge and experience that Eric has accumulated, much of it the hard way, over all of his journeys is immense and invaluable today and for the future. He has street smarts and street cred.

The reason Eric had the will to persevere, to be so adaptive, was because he had finally found that one thing on which to focus. He is going to leave literacy, for example, to David Risher and Los Angeles gang violence to Jeff Carr. Instead, Eric is so optimistic about solving the clean water problem that his goal is ending his organization's work by 2030. Splash is on track to have clean water in every orphanage in China by 2016—all 1,200 orphanages in all 31 provinces. He has a clear, realistic plan, and he has never thought of quitting. Eric says simply, "I have no desire to be anywhere else." He can't not do this.

Eric didn't find the thing that he is determinedly optimistic about until he was nearly 30 years old. His cause emerged, grew, and evolved over the years. As in Eric's case, at some point, all of what you've learned over time might mesh with the experiences you have gathered. A problem you see in the world may go from being a problem to more of a puzzle. And puzzles are solvable.

Eric left me with this thought: "I have always been a bit hesitant to start something without understanding the full scope/rules/ guardrails/and so on first. In sports, school, and in life, once I knew the parameters I dove in and went all out, normally exceeding expectations or swan diving not so gracefully, and headfirst, into concrete. Starting Splash required being okay with knowing nothing at the outset. That trend continues to this day. While I try and safeguard the organization with as much external data and internal durability as I can, we make leaps of faith all the time without knowing what the rules are. And that has become one of our greatest strengths: *not knowing the limits, we aren't encumbered by them.*" Those last nine words would be part of the manifesto of any determined optimist.

This Work Does Not Have to Be an Epic Endeavor

David and Eric completely reordered their lives based on their can't not do. While their stories are inspiring and their commitment profound, for many of us this level of commitment is unachievable. Does this mean you can't help effect change? No! I cannot stress this enough. You don't need to start your own nonprofit. You don't need to quit your job. You don't need to relocate to a third-world country. Just because you cannot do this work full-time does not mean you can't learn a heck of a lot of lessons from people who are. But regardless, you do have to find your determined optimism about one can't not do that you believe in.

Kerry McClenahan founded and owns a communications consulting firm in Portland, Oregon, and has weathered the challenging ups and downs of the economy. The company has had booms and busts and she has overseen them all. She doesn't have a lot of extra time.

Kerry is a smart and dynamic person who readily admits that, until a few years ago, she "had no idea, *no idea*," that over one-third of the five-year-olds in the Portland area show up their first day of kindergarten academically behind their peers by two years. She has two kids of her own, so it's not like she was new to the local school system. In her words, "The odds are stacked against you if you start way behind the first day you walk into school." It's not insurmountable, but it's sort of like running a marathon, giving a 10-mile head start to lots of other runners, and still trying to reach the finish line—graduate high school—at the same time.

She learned all this one night in a meeting in 2010 and said, "My consciousness changed that night." It was a "huge injustice" that she didn't know existed in her own backyard. She told me she'd never felt that kind of passion for any topic or outside interest in her life. Sometimes this stuff builds over many years; sometimes you have an epiphany one night.

When I talked to Kerry on the phone (I've met her once in person at a conference in Portland), she exuded a conviction, a purposefulness similar to Anne Reece's passion and energy. It's funny, there is a feeling I often sense when I talk with the Davids, Erics, and Kerrys of our world. I'm a little predisposed to like them, I suppose, but there is an authenticity that really comes through in all of them. They have very different personalities and causes they focus on, but the sense of their authentic selves comes across almost every time, whether it's over a cup of coffee or a phone call; Kerry was no exception.

When I asked if she believes they can meet the goal of all kids having an equal chance to learn on the first day of kindergarten, she was candid in her response. "It's impossible . . . and I won't stop until we reach that goal." She won't stop because she decided she could find a few hours a week, in between her business and kids, to become so committed. Kerry did not have to change her whole life's trajectory. She reprioritized a few things to make room for something she found more important and rewarding. She has given a few hours a week, consistently and persistently, to Portland's Ready for Kindergarten initiative, leveraging her marketing and communications skills to help that organization improve its community outreach and messaging.

If we look at our weekly schedules, can we find two or three hours of our lives to dedicate to a higher purpose? Nearly all of us can, including me. It requires some reprioritization and cleaving off less purposefully spent time to make space for something more meaningful and rewarding. Kerry did not embark on an epic endeavor spanning decades, like Andy, or continents, like Eric, but she is no less committed or less of a determined optimist than those who do. When I asked if Kerry would stick with her work for the long term, she said, "I couldn't imagine not." Could not imagine not, her exact words. It is Kerry's can't not do.

So What's Mine?

My own can't not do took some time to discover and required an embarrassing moment before I could fully embrace it. Lynann is a work colleague, a peer mentor, and a true friend. A perceptive and gifted marketer, she worked for years alongside me as an SVP partner. She tells it like it is. We were talking over a beer, one late afternoon under an August Seattle sun, and she stopped mid-sentence, out of the blue, and asked, "Do you know what you make me feel, Shoemaker?"

"Ahhh, no. What?" I asked.

"You make me feel like I matter. Yeah, you make me feel like I matter."

I paused, not knowing how to take the comment. My first reaction was to push the statement away, reject it in show of humility, but, more honestly, because it made me uncomfortable. I said dismissively, "That's flattering. But c'mon, can't be that big of a deal."

Now Lynann paused. She looked me in the eye and told me, "Damn you, Shoemaker. If you ever reject something I say like that again, after I offer something that personal from my soul, you will lose a friend." My turn for a very long pause.

Lynann offered me an exceptionally valuable lesson that day, an insight into my own gifts, which I had yet to fully accept. Although I handled the situation poorly, Lynann's words were a wake-up call. I had an ability, something I would now call a joy, for helping people see how they matter and can contribute in the world. We all have gifts, this happens to be one of mine. After our conversation I realized I needed to drop the insecurity, embrace my gift, own it, and put that talent to greater use for others. Not because I felt I had to, but because I wanted to. Wow, the power of a good friend who will tell you the truth and provide an invaluable lesson in the power of just listening.

What I can't not do in my life now is be a messenger for what I've witnessed in order to help people—as many as I humanly can—understand that there are questions that can unlock their potential to contribute and help change the world. I have a fundamental, deep faith in the purposeful power that one person like David, Eric, or Kerry can have. Having that faith gives me enormous hope and belief that we can change and solve major social problems. I know that can sound a little naive, but my belief is not transitory, superficial, or casual. It's a core, foundational belief in the power of the individual. Everything in this book starts from that place.

I'm also a good example of someone who isn't so much focused on one social issue, like the environment or poverty or education, as I am on people and helping them realize their greatest potential to create positive change in the world. That's my cause and what lights my fire most brightly and burns longest for me. I've worked side by side now with hundreds and hundreds of high-quality people, from all walks of life, to help them define a vision for themselves (to help the world, not just themselves) and a pathway to help realize it. It's one of the core things we do at SVP, and it's core to me and who I am. Let me emphasize this again: Your can't not do might not be a social issue, it might be the part of the system where you feel like you can add the most value and have the biggest impact, like leadership development, team building, connecting, or convening.

One person can start a change in the world or in a neighborhood. There is no problem that one person can't start to help solve, if that individual is determined and optimistic enough. The determined optimist goes into the challenge expecting setbacks but believing an answer is out there. I love the quote by German writer Johann Wolfgang von Goethe:

The moment one commits oneself, Providence moves, too. Whatever you can do, or dream you can do, begin it. Boldness has genius, power, and magic in it.

Be intentional about how and where you spend the "change the world" time in your life. Commit to that one thing where you have more optimism, more boldness, and begin to address it, because there is genius, power, and magic in it.

Optimism + Determination

"It completely altered my life," said Dwight Frindt, a good friend who had just hit his 70th birthday. I was casually mentioning the idea of can't not do to him over a coffee, and he told me this was his 38th year of commitment to The Hunger Project (THP). Thirty-eighth year! He had gone to listen to two people one evening in 1977 who were creating a new organization to end hunger and poverty. "It altered the work I do, even the entire methodology of the work I do," he said.

He was galvanized that evening by what he heard about the problem of hunger worldwide and the founders' belief that they could conquer it. But what was most compelling to Dwight was a little white card the founders asked each person to sign if he or she wanted to support THP (www.thp.org). It said simply the following:

> *The Hunger Project is mine completely.*
> *I am willing to be responsible*
> *for making the end of starvation*
> *an idea whose time has come.*

There is so much can't not do in those 24 words. Dwight told me, "There was no Hunger Project before I participated as I started just after it was founded in 1977. Prior to that I had volunteered for various things and made small donations. It was only when THP was launched that I saw the opportunity to change the fundamental condition in the world that leads to all of the seemingly impossible-to-alter situations like hunger, slavery, sex trade, abuse, poverty, and so on. THP was immediately exciting as it offered the possibility of altering the very condition itself rather than gesturing at the symptoms."

Over the past 38 years, Dwight has raised a family, had a few different careers, tragically lost his first wife to a car accident, and then successfully rebuilt his career and life around his leadership philosophies. Through it all, The Hunger Project has never been his full-time job, but it has been an all-consuming calling in his life. I asked him how much time he has invested, and Dwight told me, "an occasional week for a board retreat, lots of phone calls, some fund raising, being an advocate, that kind of stuff. It probably averages out to a few hours a week. Not much," he said. Do the math: 38 years × 2 hours × 52 weeks = nearly 4,000 hours. That's a full-time job for two years.

That's what the determination of can't not do looks, feels, and sounds like.

Dwight's outlook also conveys a sense of starting the end of something. Dwight might not see the endgame in his lifetime, though he tells me emphatically he will, but he has put his stake in the ground. He'll tell you his work is not about "helping starving people," it's about "the end of hunger." That powerful optimism makes it doable, even inevitable, if enough people commit as deeply as and determinedly as Dwight has. The work of a change agent takes optimism plus determination. It's the combination of the two attributes that starts the process of change. And Dwight has both.

Dwight told me more about where his optimism comes from. "The thought that the circumstances are all too overwhelming and impossible to alter creeps into my mind regularly, especially when I first visit a country or villages where hunger and poverty exist. Then I start thinking I've wasted lots of money and time. After being with the villagers, I remember that this is the only thing that can work, people unleashed and owning their own lives and futures."

I'll come back to Dwight in the Conclusion, but one of my goals is to give you the sense that these people come from all walks of life and lifestyles. Having more money and time helps, but they are not the key ingredients. Dwight is 70 and is the kind of guy who looks you in the eye all the time. He is a person who makes you feel like he has figured out life, though I'm sure he'd never say that. There is, indeed, wisdom with age and Dwight exudes that quality; you really want to do a whole lot of listening when you are with him. We almost lost him to heart failure and bypass a few years ago; I'm so thankful he is still here to do more good for the world.

Do you have to be like Dwight and give 38 years to a cause to have an impact? No. But you do have to find your optimism to change a situation and be determined enough to keep at the change long enough. If you need a rule of thumb for "long enough," I'd say at least 10 years. The personal timelines of determined optimists are much longer than other people's once they focus. They have a sort of "the heck with it, I'm gonna do this" attitude, and much of their fear and hesitation peel away and it frees up tremendous energy. There is almost a release that comes from that commitment.

= Grit

One other way to understand this whole idea is an equation: determination + optimism = grit. Pioneering psychologist Angela Lee Duckworth's work on the quality that predicts excellence more than any other centers on the notion of "grit."[4] She explains, based on years of research, "grit is the disposition to pursue very long-term goals with passion and perseverance." I want to add emphasis to the stamina quality of grit. Grit is sticking with things over the long term and working very hard at them. That's a pretty good working definition of can't not do.

Duckworth continues, "Grit is living life like it's a marathon, not a sprint." When she measured this trait to determine the likelihood of high school students graduating, it was far more significant than family income, test scores, how safe the kids felt at school, and other factors. Grit, the students' determined optimism, mattered more than anything else. In one interview, talking about her own life, Duckworth reflected that, when she was in her mid-20s, she "realized that I wasn't going to be really good at anything unless I stuck with one thing for a long time . . . shifting, sorting every two or three years was not going to add up to what I wanted."[5]

Whether you can commit a few hours a week or commit your life's work, determined optimists like Dwight, David, Eric, and Kerry are changing our world every day. What is the challenge in your world that your friends and the media may think is intractable, but you simply do not? You know the challenge can be solved. You know it is complex, but not insurmountable. What challenge are you fundamentally optimistic about in your community, in your nation, in the world that you can stick with for the long haul? Can you see any part of David, Eric, Kerry, or Dwight in you? Can you be a determined optimist?

Five Key Ideas from Chapter 1

1. You only need, preferably will have, one *can't not do* at a time in your life. Focus and go deep with intentionality if you want to have true, sustained impact. One.
2. There are some common attributes of determined optimists. They are very realistic, focused, flexible and adaptive, and have a resilient attitude.
3. You might find out what you are a determined optimist about as the result of a big epiphany or a significant, single event in your life. Or it might be something that emerges over many years. Everyone's pathway is unique.
4. Your endeavor doesn't have to be full-time. It doesn't have to be a full career commitment. I introduced you to Dwight and Kerry alongside David and Eric. What matters more is sustained focus over many years.
5. Just because you are not doing this can't-not-do work full-time does not mean you can't learn a heck of a lot of lessons from people who are.

CHAPTER 2

Lisa Chin Is Not Doing This to Be Happy

Who Are You at Your Core?

Our greatest fear is not that we are inadequate, but that we are powerful beyond measure.

It is our light, not our darkness that frightens us. We ask ourselves, Who am I to be brilliant, gorgeous, handsome, talented and fabulous? Actually, who are you not to be? You are a child of God. Your playing small does not serve the world. There is nothing enlightened about shrinking so that other people won't feel insecure around you.

We were born to make manifest the glory within us. It is not just in some; it's in everyone.

As we let our own light shine, we consciously give other people permission to do the same.

As we are liberated from our fear, our presence liberates others.

—Marianne Williamson

She is pretty matter-of-fact about taking the leap: "I was at a real crossroads in my life. I was working at a large company and I knew I didn't want to do that anymore. I didn't know what I wanted to do exactly, but I needed a change." I met Lisa Chin about 10 years ago. When you talk about thoughtful, humble, smart, she is all that in spades. At that time, she'd had a successful, 20-year career in the private sector. But she needed a change.

Around the same time, she was pregnant with a baby boy. The birth sparked something unexpected, and I don't mean a baby. "I had my moment of really believing in myself when I had Benjamin. It wasn't the college degrees. It wasn't the job titles. It was in giving birth to a child. It was a powerful experience and made me think 'wow, if every woman had this kind of confidence, that moment of really believing in herself, look what I just did.' It made me want to help other people feel that strong sense of *empowerment*. And then I thought my God, what about all the moms who don't have as many resources. If they had this, it could change their lives and their babies' lives in incredible ways. So I went for it." Lisa found the work that is about a core sense of self and she found that level of passion and commitment from an unexpected place, because she was open to the possibilities at that point in her life.

I went by her office last year to spend a few hours with her, 19- and 20-year-olds streaming in and out as we talked. She radiated an interesting combination of deep compassion and no-nonsense. I'd want her on my side in just about any fight—both because she'd care deeply, and also because I wouldn't want to be on the other side. In all the years I've done this work, few people have become more trusted, valued, honest colleagues than Lisa. She is also, by the way, a determined optimist in spades.

Lisa joined Open Arms Perinatal Services (www.openarmsps.org) as the executive director. The organization helps increase awareness of how doulas are an important and empowering link in supporting early learning. She then went on to head up Jubilee Women's Center (www.jwcenter.org) which empowers homeless women by providing transitional housing. Right now, she is the executive director of Year Up Seattle (www.yearup.org), a nonprofit that provides urban young adults with the skills, experience, and support that will empower them to reach their potential through professional careers and higher education. Eighty-five percent of Year Up graduates are employed or attending college full-time within four months of completing the year-long program. When you look in the dictionary, next to the word "empowerment," there is surely a picture of Lisa. It is part of her core being. It is just who she is.

Gerald Chartavian is the founder, CEO, and leader of the national Year Up model and movement; his can't not do is very contagious, one of the key attributes of determined optimists we talked about in Chapter 1. Lisa is one of those people that caught the bug of trying to help 6.7 million opportunity youth (explained at http://bit.ly/188yUib) succeed in college and life; they've reached tens of thousands so far, and Gerald and Lisa will tell you they have lots of work left to do.[1] I love the audacity of, authentic belief in, and unbridled commitment to their goals. And the reason they believe that such an audacious, some would say outrageous, goal is doable is because of those social multipliers at play in our world, combined with can't-not-do people like Gerald and Lisa.

I talked with Lisa about what some of her toughest moments have been. She told me about one Year Up participant who was homeless, sleeping in his car because his family kicked him out of the house and then mental health problems sent him into a downward spiral. Lisa said, "There were times when he was in my office, lost, terrified, and in tears, and I just wanted to find him a new home. Doing this work really challenges my boundaries, my own identity and capacity to love. I've grown up quite a bit, had my own 'year up.'"

People ask her now, "Are you happy?" Lisa says, "I have to think for a moment because for me it's not about doing this to be happy. I completely believe in what I'm doing and who I am and that to me is far more fulfilling than 'are you happy?' I'm not unhappy at all. It's the bigger sense of purpose where you just know. I once told my students that if somebody came in here with a gun, I would step in front of it for them. You feel like what you're doing is the right thing to do right now."

It's interesting to ponder exactly what is Lisa's can't not do. Is it empowering people? Or helping young adults? Both are good, but understanding your own underlying core beliefs does matter. I suspect with Lisa it's more about the sense of empowerment that she feels so passionate about enabling in others, but maybe that has evolved into a tighter focus on empowering young adults now. We'll see in the years ahead, but it's also an important reminder that your can't not do can evolve. It might be subtle like Lisa's, or more completely into a new realm altogether, after you've committed to one cause for a sustained period in a deep way (remember, I said 10 years is a good rule of thumb for a sustained period of time).

There was one last thing Lisa told me that day at her office. Leaving to pick up now nine-year-old Benjamin after school, Lisa paused and said, unprompted and I quote, "It's not that I can do this work, Shoe, it's that I can't not." *It's not that I can, I can't not.* I think she was the first of now many people who I've heard utter that head-twisting phrase.

What's the Point?

Core beliefs are fundamental to who you are. They reflect what you truly believe about yourself and your world. They form the internal compass that guides you. The idea of your work, your cause, being connected to your core is about knowing what makes you who you are. It's about optimizing what you are good at.

In sports, people talk about the contrast between players who "let the game come to them" versus "force the action." There is a role for both kinds of players and coaches, but maybe nobody personifies the former concept more than the guy who made one of the most iconic shots in NBA history.

Ray Allen, the all-time greatest three-point shooter in NBA history, is known for getting a "quiet 25 points." He gets a feel for the game, picks his spots. He lets the game come to him, like in game six of the 2013 NBA finals when he buried a beyond-improbable three-pointer at the buzzer that "spurred" (pun intended) Miami on to an NBA championship over the San Antonio Spurs. Allen knows what he is good at, he's practiced what he is good at over and over again. He's hit that shot in his mind's eye many times before he actually took the one that mattered. At that moment, he knew where to find an open spot based on what was going on around him and when the shot came to him, he nailed it; sorry, Spurs fans. There is a serenity to Allen's game that comes not just from his physical attributes and style of play, but from a clear, strong sense of what he is, and is not, great at on the court.

Like many of the most powerful change agents in the world today, the great players have a focus and passion that comes from something deeply connected to who they are, and that optimizes what they are the very best at. Why tell basketball stories? Because understanding who you are at your core is about each of us letting the game come to us, finding that cause that fits our talents, that fits fluidly into our lifestyle and passions. I can, unequivocally, say that about SVP and my life. Another reason for sharing a basketball story is to illustrate the ideas of core belief and determined optimism in a different way through a different walk of life that might resonate more deeply with you.

David Risher's passion was deeply rooted in his core love of books, which he has had since he was five years old. Would someone less in love with books see the problem the way he did? For others, the cause might take longer to find. What does matter is that your cause is connected to who you are at your core. Because it will play to your talents and passions most intensely; it will feel natural when it comes to you, like the pass that came to Ray Allen in the corner. When your one cause is connected to your core, you will give more to it, more freely, and with greater effort, time and, ultimately, reward and impact.

A Cause Connected to Your Core for Someone Else

"When we first came to America, it was very difficult. I think that really affected the way that I think about the world." Vu Le was born in Vietnam and moved to the United States with his family when he was eight years old. He went to elementary school in Seattle and then moved to Memphis where his family started a business. He told me, "My parents, like a lot of immigrant families, wanted to own a small business. It's a good way to control things, be their own boss. It's a very symbolic thing." Vu is a fun guy, also passionate and blunt, almost to a fault. He likes to mix it up. He has this way of looking at you earnestly with a smile on his face and delivering a tough, honest message at the same time. I love working with people like Vu.

He grew up experiencing the challenges of immigration with parents who didn't know how to navigate the new culture or speak the new language. He remembers what it was like being a kid and figuring out systems that were confusing and tasks as ordinary as homework without a lot of support from parents who spoke very little English. He talked a little bit about the experiences that shaped his life. "I knew I wanted to do something that would be helpful to the community, and I think that is because of my upbringing, going through immigration and all the challenges my parents went through."

After college, like Eric Stowe, Vu wandered for a few years, not knowing where he should land or what he should do. No matter where he went or what he did, he always had the same mantra running through his mind: "How can I be helpful to my community?" That is core to who Vu is and how he sees the world.

He ended up back in Seattle, working with the Vietnamese Friendship Association (www.vfaseattle.org), an organization started in 1978 to help refugees and immigrants resettle in the United States. It was a bit of a full circle. Vu knows how hard things are when the deck is stacked against you. He talks about the kids he sees at one of the Saturday English classes the association runs: "Half of them don't speak much English yet, most of them are low-income, and few have language support from their families at home because their parents work two or three jobs to try to make ends meet or have little knowledge of the school system. We know from current statistics that half of these new-arrival students will not graduate from high school. We work with the school and other nonprofits to try to stem the tide, but there will always be kids whose futures remain uncertain."

Vu feels VFA is where he is supposed to be. He told me he "wanted to do something great with my life, to go where I am needed." To go where you are needed is all about being connected to your core. It's about optimizing your talents and life experiences. Vu asks himself again and again, "How would I have helped someone in my situation?" That is an awesome perspective, selfless, forward-looking, a real determination within. *How would I have helped someone in my situation?* Remember that one; it feels sort of like the Golden Rule.

Vu needed determination when he started at VFA. When he joined, he not only faced the challenges of running a nonprofit, he faced some real hurdles within his own community. To the important elders of the community, many of whom felt the lingering effects of the war in which they fought, Vu was just a young whippersnapper. The elders had lost so much stature in coming to the United States where their professional credentials and experiences were not valued. VFA was their baby and Vu was just an unruly upstart kid who didn't know much. After a bumpy start, Vu stepped back. He started to take more time to get to know people and to listen to their stories.

Vu told me he had to change. He had to learn a lot more about what he *didn't* know than what he *did* know (see Chapter 5, Humble and Humbled). Through all that, because he let his cause come to him, he learned how to be a voice for his community.

In Vu's words, "As an immigrant kid whose family went through a lot—war, reeducation camp, migration to a new land with no language skills or jobs—I always felt this guilt for following my passion. For a long time I would think, it's not too late for me to be a doctor and make my parents proud, make our relatives that we left behind proud, too. Once I committed to this path of community organizing and nonprofit leadership, I had to learn to live with the guilt, and also the doubts, and the complete bewilderment and confusion from my family. No one in my family understands what I'm doing, even to this day. I have to be okay with that and to accept that this, at least in the short-term, is part of the price of doing what I feel I'm meant to do." Vu is living in accordance with something very deep in his core.

If you look back through Vu's life experiences, becoming the executive director of VFA might seem obvious, but for many years, especially in his 20s, it didn't. Sometimes it's hard to see the forest for the trees when you are so immersed in it. Eventually he listened, looked around, and ended up in a place where he could optimally apply his talents and skills to be, as he desired, most helpful to his community.

Now, before you start thinking that Vu is this saintly kind of guy who sits calmly behind a desk trying to solve world problems, you should also know he writes one of the most irreverent nonprofit blogs in existence (www.nonprofitwithballs.com). He does crazy things like auctioning off the right to choose the middle name of his newborn or have a bathroom stall named after you (like the one that's named for me) in order to raise funds for VFA. His LinkedIn profile kind of says it all: "Vu's passion to make the world better, combined with a low score on the Law School Admission Test, drove him into the field of nonprofit work. Known for his no-BS approach, irreverent sense of humor, and love of unicorns, Vu has been featured in dozens, if not hundreds, of his own blog posts. . . . "

Whether in his blog posts, his work with the elders, the nonprofit musical he's writing (seriously), or working in the community, Vu is a role model for someone who is doing something deeply connected to he is at his core. In his case, it's his upbringing and ethnicity. He wrote a beautiful blog post (http://bit.ly/1M2MFw1) about Bill Hennings-gaard after we lost him back in August 2013, just another poignant way in which the people in this book are connected. One more thing Vu told me, "If you want to do something great, you've got to give up some of the romance, you know. You should be where you're needed, not where you think is the sexiest place to be." What's at *your* core that you want to do something about in this world?

The Right Time and Place

Discovering or affirming who you are at your core requires being extremely honest with yourself, taking the time to be self-reflective, enlisting good friends and colleagues who know you well and can perhaps see things you don't see as readily in yourself. Here's a quick checklist you can use:

- *What is in my roots when I trace back through the early years of my life?* Maybe your family used to do a lot of camping and being outdoors when you were young so you'll be more passionate about and connected to environmental causes. What kinds of things did you talk about as a family that you remember most vividly? What did you most admire, or not, about your parents and siblings? All of these are potential guideposts, any of which just might help lead you to who you are at your core.
- *When I look back through my life, what experiences along the way had the most effect on who I am today?* Look, for example, at David Risher. He

didn't seek out or plan for what happened at that orphanage. However, when it did, it was a short distance for him to travel back to being a reader growing up and translate that into a desire to eradicate illiteracy. He saw a situation and used his life experiences as a powerful reference point that led him to a vital decision for the course of his life. If it hadn't been that orphanage, I believe there would have been another triggering event at some point in his life. In that summer of 2004, David was open and the cause connected with what is core to him.

- *If I looked at this like getting a new job or joining a team, what landing spot would best use my skills, experiences, talents?* What does Starbucks have to do with curing corneal blindness? There are few more successful examples of franchising around the world than Starbucks. Tim Schottman got the connection almost immediately. In his role of director of global strategy, Tim helped Starbucks grow from 100 local stores to 15,000 stores in more than 44 countries. He was definitely an expert at scaling businesses. SightLife (www.sightlife .org), whose mission is to alleviate corneal blindness around the world, was doing great work, but desperately needed to scale its operations. While the supply of good corneas continually improves, SightLife had few reliable supply chains to get the corneal tissue where it was most needed around the world. It was a classic scaling-up challenge.

SightLife needed to replicate Starbucks' worldwide growth strategy, and there were few people more qualified than Tim to help. All that was left to do was to get Tim's heart connected and that didn't take very long once SightLife found him. What someone learned about growing a coffee company is going to enable thousands, someday millions of people to get their eyesight back. Tim was at a point in his life when he was open to possibilities. He found the landing spot in life that used his talents, and eventually passion, exceedingly well.

And how'd it work out? Here's what SightLife's website says, "Each day, we restore sight in more than 50 men, women, and children globally. This is a direct result of working with eye banks and surgeons in dozens of countries. . . . By sharing our industry-leading approach with our global partners, we're helping to build successful local corneal transplant programs around the world." Think of the simple, profound life-changing moment that happens every 30 minutes somewhere around the world. Just stop and feel how good that feels for a minute; that's what Tim's can't not do is doing for the world.

- *When I think about the future and finding some pursuit to change the world, what avenues affect me in the most visceral, instinctual way? What sends that chill up my spine?* Jeff Carr, who you met earlier, had a career based in social justice and community work. He spent 17 years in Los Angeles working with youth and afterschool programs in that city. During that time, he made connections with civic organizations, police, schools, and the city council. He also got to know the kids, the neighborhoods, and the challenges.

He eventually got restless, as he put it, he could feel the winds of change blowing around him (I know that sounds a little corny). So when the right idea came along, to help reduce gang violence in Los Angeles in a significant and profoundly different way, it was as if his life had been preparing him for this moment, for this cause to find him, like Ray Allen in the corner. He became the city's first deputy mayor for gang reduction and youth development. Everything he'd learned, the relationships he built, and the faith he had in young people all came to bear when he took on the role. Jeff knew he had to do it. He couldn't not do it.

In all of these instances, the cause intersected with each person at an opportune time in their lives. Inherent in this idea is being open to a cause finding you in the first place. Vu needed a job and was open to all sorts of possibilities. Jeff felt the winds of change and knew it was time for something different. When SightLife reached out to Tim, he was open for a different challenge. We are all more or less open at different stages of our lives. There are times in life when change fits and other times when it just doesn't. Just be listening to yourself and the world around you along the way in life so you don't miss it.

Quite often, your can't not do will appear at a transition point in life—when you move into a new town, once all the kids are in school, something changes and you have more time on your hands, you are ready for something new and meaningful in your life, you have a lingering feeling or an itch to scratch. I hope using the seven questions in this book helps you be more ready to find a cause connected to your core self.

When I was working on how to talk about core, I e-mailed back and forth with my friend, Larry Fox, and more than once I saved a few things he said like, "Caring is actually hard, it can be a burden, it brings with it responsibility. It makes us vulnerable to disappointment and loss, and that's why it is essential for us as individuals to reflect on our values, goals, and behavior. It is important to reconnect with and reestablish what we stand for at our core; it is important to stimulate our courage, to encourage ourselves, and to feel the full weight of what it means to care and to recommit to the work it requires of us, from our core."

Your time and resources have the potential to make a profound impact on the world. Remember the idea about only needing to find that one thing you are a determined optimist about? Too many people commit too much of their time and resources to something that doesn't come from—and isn't deeply connected to—who they are at their core. Your time matters. Lives can be saved and enriched. The sooner the right cause finds you, the sooner you can make a long-term commitment and the more good you can do for the world.

Putting Optimism to Work: $1 + 1 + 1 + 1 = 10$

I answered this question about what is core for me rather unintentionally, at first. As I mentioned earlier, my dad was a Methodist minister while I was growing up. The last thing I want to do in this world is be a minister, and I don't believe there is a divinity school in the country that would accept me; God would send a hailstorm upon any school that would.

But I was there, all those years growing up, watching my dad do his thing. He was a man of faith, no doubt. But more than that, I think he was a man of connection. He loved being in the middle of the action and figuring out who needed to know who and when and why and then making the connections happen.

The strength of a church is highly correlated with the quality and quantity of connections between the members. That was true 40 years ago, it is true today, and will be for the next 400 years. And it is true for many institutions, not just the church. All of that is to say I must have been paying attention, watching what he did and how he did it, because connecting people is what I've been doing the last 17 years. It's most certainly where I came from and it's who I am today. It's the game that fits my skills and experiences. It's who I am at my core, though it took me half my life to see it. And now I live in a world of far greater social multipliers, so those connections are more and more valuable with each passing day.

I recognized, over time, how my mind would work when I went into a meeting or sat down with a new person, one to one. I would start doing this sort of networking and connecting thing, like my dad did, without even realizing it. My mind would go to things like, who would this person want to know or be connected to that would help her achieve her goals? Who else out there has common challenges or problems and could help her and be helped in turn? Who were the other three people that asked me just about the same question during the last month, and can I get the four of them together? What is the

1 + 1 that isn't connected, but should be? And where is the $1 + 1 = 3$ connection out there waiting to happen? There is a sort of matrix, a network map going on in my head all the time; that is the fun of the job. That is where the potential for real change is. (See Chapter 6, Do You Believe $1 + 1 = 3$? to learn more about connections.)

Sometimes a cause finds you when you're not even looking for it. Sometimes it's out there and it takes about 40 years to find an important part of who you are at your core. Maybe I was, in fact, born to do this . . . yep, that feels right to me now.

Five Key Ideas from Chapter 2

1. Talk to others and ask them what defines you. Talk to several people who have different experiences and vantage points, take notes and ask for feedback. And then sit down with your notes and reflections and see what patterns emerge that might lead to what you feel truly determined and optimistic about at your core.

2. Look at your roots, trace back through the early years of your life, and think about what people made you who you are today.

3. Look back through your adult years: what experiences along the way had the most effect on who you are today? Look for common themes and threads that would lead you to a cause where you can feel truly committed for the right reasons and for the long term.

4. Think about the future. What pathway to helping change the world affects you in the most visceral, instinctual way? What sends that chill up your spine and really grabs your heart as well as your head?

5. Reflect back on the stories about Lisa and Vu; was there anything from their stories that really resonated for you? As you talk to others, ask them not only for feedback about you, but also ask what they think is core for their life. What can you learn from listening to someone else talk about his or her life? And you can practice listening well, too, while you're at it.

CHAPTER 3

Eleuthera Lisch, Stepping Out from Behind the Fourth Wall

Are You Willing to Go to Hard Places?

It is always wise to look ahead, but difficult to look further than you can see.

—Winston Churchill

The "fourth wall" in theater is an imaginary wall that stands between the actors on stage and the audience. Actors pretend they can't see the audience and the audience gets to play the quiet voyeur. The actors entertain, but they don't interact. The audience gets to watch, but they can't influence. It's a weird dynamic, but it satisfies both parties. Stepping out from behind the wall breaks the detachment.

Eleuthera Lisch has been a professional actor since early childhood. She explained the concept of the fourth wall to me as "the blackness in which you are pretending this is real. So the audience is watching something and the actors are pretending that the audience isn't there. When you bust past that fourth wall, it is a raw human interaction."

I know you might be thinking, since when is the theater a hard place? For Eleuthera, the theater itself wasn't the hard place. Taking her theater training into a detention center filled with violent criminals was. It was a way for her to give back through her talents. And, it was what set her on the path to some even harder places.

There is a form of therapy that encourages inmates to write monologues from the perspective of their victims. It is saying to them, "go to the place of empathy where you become the person you chose to murder." On one of her visits, Eleuthera challenged them to try on what it feels like to be the victim. That fourth wall came crashing down for Eleuthera one day during an inmate's performance of her monologue. She could no longer separate herself from the violence she was hearing about. The experience hit very close to home for Eleuthera. It was one of those pivot points in life.

Violence had played a major role in her early life. She calls it a "generational legacy that I inherited from my brilliant and complicated parents." Time and time again, her familiarity with and acceptance of violence led her directly to danger. By the time she was 17, she had run away to Amsterdam and started trafficking drugs. She was alone and lost in a foreign country where she got kidnapped, sexually assaulted, and left by the side of the road. The compassion and empathy of strangers was the only thing that saved her.

Eleuthera gave an amazing talk at TEDxRainier (www .tedxrainier.org) in 2013. It is powerful, intense, and, at times, hard for me to listen to . . . and nothing even remotely like what it must have been to live through it, of course. But if you want to know more about why my convictions about her grew even stronger, take 10 minutes and Google her performance at TEDx.

Eleuthera's can't not do was to no longer look the other way when it came to violence and the impact it had. Today, she is deeply committed to the prevention of youth violence and ridding our culture of the disease of violence. When the Seattle Police Department has to respond to a youth or gang-related shooting, she is often one of the first people they call. They get her on site to deal with the immediate human ramifications and sometimes to help strategize how to prevent the spread of more violence in the aftermath. She hears things from youth on the street like, "I am telling you because I am building trust with you, but if anyone finds out I told you, I'm dead. If anybody finds out what you know right now, you're dead. And if you do this wrong, someone else is dead."

She told me that solving the issue of violence is like solving a Rubik's Cube. You know the answer is there, you just have to keep turning the sides. She will tell you, "Youth violence is solvable, there is no doubt about that. It is just how many steps and how quickly and what am I doing that gets in my own way before I can actually get it done." There is an underlying determined optimism within her that just won't go away and this cause is deeply connected to Eleuthera's core.

She is one of the more unique human beings I've ever met. For starters, how do you have a childhood like hers and still find it in your heart to not only forgive but make ending violence a part of your career? That takes a special kind of person. She has an earthy, grounded, deeply authentic quality to her.

Eleuthera is clearly an exceptional example of how far someone will go to help solve a social problem. I don't think she knows what's not possible. No, you don't have to hit the streets, like she literally did, to prove you are willing to go to the hard places. That's not the point. Like I said in the introduction, just because we aren't Martin Luther King, Jr. or Gandhi or Rosa Parks doesn't mean we can't learn a lot and apply vital life lessons from their examples. Just because you or I didn't live Eleuthera's life doesn't mean we can't learn a lot from her. The point is to ask yourself questions like, "What is my fourth wall?"

"What cause would make me willing, figuratively or literally, to hit the streets, to go to hard places?"

An important footnote here: last year, Eleuthera had to shift gears. She was burnt out from many years of work on the street. It was intense, vitally important work, but we all have our breaking point; in her case, almost literally. She rested, recuperated, and today is no less committed to the ultimate cause and purpose. Eleuthera has now shifted into more of a mentoring and advocacy role, including visits to the White House. She provides another great example of how one's can't not do will shift gears and change form at times over the years but still remain connected to one's core.

What's the Point?

When you have dug into what you believe you can't not do, the hard places are sure to follow. Going to the hard places is where you find the real challenges, the real people, the real world. It is where your commitment is tested. And there is no better way to prove your commitment than to put yourself in a challenging, hard place to see how it feels. Can you be effective when the going gets tough? Can you persevere for the long haul despite the odds and the obstacles?

Pete Carroll is the coach of the Seattle Seahawks. I didn't like him so much when he was at the University of Southern California, but I love him now that he's our coach and I have a much better sense of the whole person. When he's not working the sidelines, his greatest passion is preventing youth and gang violence. He created A Better LA (www.abetterla.org) to "restore peace, save lives, and give Angelenos living in inner city LA the resources they need in order to thrive." He also created A Better Seattle (www.abetterseattle.com) to "reduce Seattle area youth and gang violence by forging partnerships that generate opportunities for at-risk youth to take control of their lives and strive for better futures."

Any time I see a sports star, Hollywood star, or famous personality create a charitable endeavor, I am skeptical. So does Pete Carroll really mean business or is he just building his image? Well, one way to know is to ask if he has been willing to go, literally, to the hard places. To go on the street to meet these young people where they are. And does he do it when the cameras aren't rolling?

The answer is a definite yes (he did take *60 Minutes* with him one evening in Los Angeles to draw attention to the issue). He's out there, many nights, in the middle of the night, when the spotlight isn't on. No, Pete Carroll is not putting his life at risk, simply because of who he is. But he is going where the real problem lives. He is finding the hard places, and the youth there, and vows he'll continue once the spotlights fade.

I happened to be in a working session last year that focused on A Better Seattle. We knew Coach Carroll was going to stop in for a few minutes. He was there on time, stayed beyond his scheduled time, and talked as passionately about this work as I'd ever seen him talk about a football game. And that means a very high, intense level of passion.

As he was getting up to leave, something made me blurt out, "So, are you truly committed to this work for the long-term, coach, meaning after you're done coaching?" After he stared me down like I was Jim Harbaugh (if you don't understand that reference, Google their two names together), he said something like, "Yes. Yes, I am. This is my passion, these kids," then he walked out, somewhat defiantly, as if my question irritated him. Time will tell, but I'd bet on him.

Coach Carroll is not a no-name, regular guy; he's pretty famous. But the lesson to learn here is universal. This is not about winning a Super Bowl. This is about going to hard places, regardless of who you are or what you have done, and sticking with it.

Look at a few of the hard places we have seen so far: third-world illiteracy, impoverished orphanages, inner city violence, the list goes on and on. These are physically and mentally hard places. Yet, there are people who are willing to go there. They are compelled to act, and if they don't, real change is much less likely to happen.

We know they are optimistic about change. They feel, in their core, that the cause needs them and they are willing to throw themselves into the fray. They know they don't have all the answers. Sometimes it's not as much about succeeding today as it is committing to the struggle for the future. Each can't-not-do person I talked with knows digging deeply into this work will sometimes be very hard, but it's the only place where real change happens. In fact, *until you make this work hard, you are probably not close enough to the real problems to help effect real change;* I can't emphasize that enough.

■   ■   ■

Does this work go smoothly? No. Failures and missteps abound. You have to be willing to deal with them. Virtuoso violinists are known for leaning in to their mistakes. When there is a piece they are struggling to play at the level to which they are accustomed, they stay with the discomfort of their failings longer than just about anyone else.[1] It is in those moments, days, and weeks of trying to get it right that they become great. They don't move on to their next piece or one that is easier or one they know they can play. They stay in that hard place.

Nowadays, we love to glorify and celebrate the tech entrepreneur who went through hell, failed and got back up, beat the odds, and succeeded. We even talk about "failing fast." Why should it be any different in this work of helping make the world a better place? What cause in life are you willing to fail and get back up for and keep on going to beat the odds and succeed?

Failure is the way we learn and get better, right? We need to reconstruct our relationship to failure, like virtuoso violinists and entrepreneurs, and rethink the role it plays in helping make each of us a better, stronger person for change in our communities. Without the willingness to fail, which is what inevitably happens when we dig into the hard places in the work of social change, real change will not happen. One way to know if you've dug in far enough is to know that failure feels likely on the horizon. That's the place where the world's best violinists and entrepreneurs, and regular heroes, lean in.

Some Hard Places Aren't Places

Kids in foster care suffer from post-traumatic stress disorder[2] at a higher rate than returning combat war veterans and more than half struggle with mental health challenges stemming from the trauma they've endured. Academically, they face an uphill battle due to changes in home placements and school transitions and the ongoing emotional upheaval. Access to important socialization opportunities, like music lessons and team sports, is limited, as is access to funding for essential needs like clothing, shoes, school supplies, haircuts, and school fees.

Let's talk about one of those agencies that tends to make the news too frequently; they don't want to either, by the way. The Washington State Department of Social and Health Services over-sees the foster care system in the state of Washington. On any given day there are 1,300 to 1,500 children in foster care in King County, and about 10,000 children in foster care across Washington state.[3] Approximately 65 percent of the kids enter the system due to parental neglect, while most of the others enter because of physical and sexual abuse. These kids come from any and all cultural, geographic, and socioeconomic groups.

There may be no more difficult, hard-to-navigate, fraught-with-entrenched-players system in our communities than the child welfare system. No doubt, you can make a meaningful contribution to the lives of individual children and youth, one at a time, but it doesn't change the underlying system. Helping one youth at a time is hard enough, and a *good* thing, but trying to change the system to help thousands of these kids live better lives demands the willingness, fortitude, thick skin, and huge heart to wade into the hard places of the child welfare system.

It's important to know that each of the regular heroes in this book brings vastly different resources and experiences to impact social problems. Some are nonprofit leaders who make change happen on the ground, and some are philanthropists who are making deep investments in their communities. Some are working the mean streets; others' hard places are monolithic agencies and governmental systems.

Connie Ballmer is one of those individuals. After reading heartbreaking articles and learning about the fate of many foster care children, she reached out to the University of Washington School of Social Work Dean Edwina Uehara and then-Department of Social and Health Services Secretary Robin Arnold-Williams to figure out what could be done and how. When I asked her what made her jump into this particular area she said, "Being a mom. Empathy with children who have no choice in this situation they're put in. I don't know why you wouldn't care. It's just such a crappy, crappy situation. For most kids, yeah, it's kind of tough if you have a bad teacher. Maybe your education isn't great that year. But it's *really* bad if you don't have a family. So to me, it feels like a no-brainer." It doesn't feel like a no-brainer to most of the rest of us.

I could have included Connie in Chapter 1 (determined optimists) very easily. Connie is one of the most grounded, centered people I've met along this journey. She refuses to take herself too seriously, is constantly open to learning and new ideas, and at the same time, just dogged in pursuit of what's right. She's going to need all of those traits. Connie provided some of the seed money to start Partners for Our Children (www.partnersforourchildren.org) to focus resources and expertise on the state's child welfare system. It is a collaboration between the Washington State Department of Social and Health Services, the University of Washington School of Social Work, and private sector and philanthropic funding. This is hard-core systems work. A lot of people get in at that level and don't realize just how hard, messy, and complex it is.

So what does the experience of diving deep enough to truly be working in a hard place like the child welfare system feel like? I'll let Connie answer that question, just read and feel what she says about her can't not do:

- *What's the mindset you need to have?* "We have to do this, just hold out. At some point you get too far into it, then you can't pull out. Well, you can pull out, but what would that say? 'Okay, we're closing up shop? It was a bad idea? We decided not to do this?' No, it's not a bad idea. It was a good idea. It is still a good idea. Somebody at the end of the line can add up how much you spend on it and go, really, was that really worth it? But for now, we are going to keep at it."
- *What keeps you going?* "There are little points of light, you know. You just need little bits of hope that can help you keep going. If we can do something, if that bit of work helps three case workers have an aha or if I can get the tech guys to upgrade the equipment so people are more efficient, then I have done something. . . . As long as we keep doing *something*."
- *And what might you learn, how might you personally be changed?* "I'm much more patient about the reality. It introduced me to the complexities of this problem, which opens my mind to being much more aware of the complexity of every issue. It's so complex. It enables me to see many more areas in gray. That's what's good about this. Because it can be a little overwhelming, but being more patient also enables you to be more effective."

Listening to Connie made me think about Lisa Chin's answer when someone asked her, "Are you happy?"

I want to be very clear about one thing—money matters, most surely. Some of the people I talked with for this book have meaningful financial resources, and some do not. But all the money in the world doesn't make one cent of difference without the persistent, dogged willingness to keep wading into the hard places. Not one cent. Connie understands the realities of being involved at this level (and she is another one of those people that is deeply focused and committed, but it's not her full-time endeavor).

"Systems work is important. Somebody's got to care about the systems. Whether it's in child welfare or just in government in general. You can't just make an end run. This is our system. These are our children." She understands and does not shy away from the hard places.

The foster/child welfare system is one of the hardest realms of all in which to make positive progress. Partners for Our Children has succeeded in being a key player in passing legislation to move toward performance-based contracting in Washington state, that is, aligning funding with successful placements of foster kids. It has also implemented a first-of-its kind data sharing arrangement with the state's Children's Administration. Pretty wonky sounding stuff, but vital precursors to seeing the same kind of progress in foster care as we've seen for reducing teen pregnancy and violent crime in the United States.

What If You Have to Leave a Hard Place?

No matter how hard we try or how committed we are, there is always a possibility that we can't stick with it. So what happens when someone decides they don't want to be in that hard place anymore? The simple fact is some people will quit; it doesn't make them bad people. Face it, each of us might be the one bailing someday. Or maybe we just need a break. Creating true, deep, and real change in our world is hard work. It can be painful and ego-bruising. Those realities leave me with a few thoughts to share:

- Before you find that cause that you really want to dig into deeply, take inventory. What's up in the rest of your life, your work, and your relationships? Do you have the personal capacity right now to invest X hours a week and enough energy and emotion for the long term? The timing in your life may not be right, so wait. But don't wait too long, and don't give yourself an easy out, either.

- If you've decided you are ready to dig in to that hard place, think about how and who will support and replenish your energy. It's going to be hard when you get close enough to the real work and the real opportunities for change. It will drain you. It will challenge your confidence. Who will be your trusted allies? Who will you turn to and who will listen? What will get you through the darkest moments and re-inspire you, like Dwight when he visits the villagers again? Have a personal support plan.

- If you do decide, for whatever reason, that you need to step back from the challenge at hand, please think about the hole you may be leaving. Before you leave, can you fill that hole with someone or something else? We could way overdo the battle analogies here, but is there someone who can pick up the fight if you have to leave the battle? Maybe you are wounded and just need a break.

- And last, but not least, you are not an evil or bad or faulty person if you do step back, especially if you've given it your honest hard work, your best effort, your authentic sweat equity. You are human. If you did give it a sincere effort, and make sure you truly did, don't beat yourself up. Be proud that you had the guts to wade in where most people won't ever go in the first place. Life around us changes, puts other pressures or demands on us. Know that maybe, just maybe, you moved the boulder up the hill just a little further, just enough so the next person can push it over the top and real change will happen.

Changing the world is not an easy task. Projects go sideways, funding dries up, politics and personalities try the patience of even the greatest of saints. Face it, failure inevitably happens along the way. And it can be a bitter pill to swallow. It can also be the source of profound lessons learned and lay the groundwork for even more satisfying, meaningful positive change down the road.

Failure Never Feels Good to Anyone, Including Me

Since 1997, SVP Seattle has worked closely with over 75 nonprofits in the greater Seattle area. When I say closely, I mean we work hand-in-hand with each nonprofit's executive director, staff, and board. We provide unrestricted grants to help a nonprofit build its organizational capacity to deliver its programs. This translates into things like building databases, developing strategic plans, negotiating leases or licensing agreements, and leadership development for key personnel. SVP assigns a single partner, an unpaid volunteer member of SVP, to work directly with the nonprofit's executive director. The partner is a sounding board, mentor, and resource locator. When the executive director and partner click, it is a beautiful thing.

But as in any relationship, there are bumps along the way. Sometimes you work them out, and sometimes the bumps are really ramps leading to a big cliff. I've watched a few of these during my tenure and they can be incredibly painful. In 2007, SVP and Passages Northwest (http://ymcaleadership.com/gold/) started a new relationship. For the first two years, we all described it as ideal. Their executive director was fully engaged in an open and honest relationship, the organization was tearing through capacity building projects and engaging with multiple SVP Partners. Its Girls Rock![4] program expanded by 40 percent, which meant more than 130 girls could take advantage of an intensive 10-week courage and leadership building class revolving around rock climbing. The young girls come back from these trips on fire with creative and physical courage.

So why is this story in the chapter on hard places? In May of 2009, the executive director tendered her resignation, effective in October. SVP has seen a lot of executive director transitions over the years and offered the services of an executive search consultant to assist the board with the process. For the first round of the search, Passages recruited a diverse search committee of board members, staff, and community stakeholders. The search committee narrowed the field to two final candidates. The board and the staff strongly disagreed on the candidates. The search committee chair, who was a board member, dismissed the candidates and fired the community stakeholders and the staff from the search committee. Board members felt that the community members and staff were not asking the right questions and didn't know how to properly evaluate an executive.

At the same time, the board started making organizational changes. It let the development director go. The board also decided to eliminate the director tier, flattening the organization and demoting those who once served in that capacity. The board and staff not only disagreed on candidates, they also disagreed on how to interpret the organization's mission. Staff felt social justice should drive who could participate in programs, and the board just wanted to get as many girls in the program as possible. Where was SVP all this time? We were paying for the executive search and knew a successful hire would mean a continued successful relationship. We were so confident in the organization's past performance, we thought that stepping back and letting the board do its work was the best approach. We also shifted our lead partner onto another project. We ended up with an angry board driving the bus, a supportive SVP partner no longer involved, and disenchanted staff wondering what the heck was going on.

By the time the board hired a new executive director in October, everyone was burned out. The organization was in financial crisis. In the end, Passages Northwest had to close its doors. The good news is the YMCA picked up its programming, but regardless, a lot of opportunity to serve more girls had been lost.

That experience went in the failure column in my book. When you add it all up, lots of people own responsibility, but I sit here knowing SVP should have seen some of this coming. We are the ones with the experience in executive director transitions and all the things that can go wrong, but I somehow stood by and watched too many things going too wrong. Nonprofits are the experts at delivering their programs; SVP is the expert guide in building organizational capacity. We kept our mouths shut when we should have been speaking up. That hurts. Living in the hard place of feeling like you failed an organization is not a comfortable feeling. Sometimes in this work, you flat-out fail and you've just got to learn.

I share that short story in the spirit of openness and owning my failure and also to show, once more, that you can't make real change unless you get close enough to the real problem. In this case, I think we were a little too afraid to get close *enough* and the consequences were significant.

Finding Meaning in a Hard Place

That whole notion that you learn more from your failures and when times are tough is so true. It's just that it sucks when you are in the middle of the mess. But most surely, you cannot know what you are made of, how committed you are, what it is you can't not do unless you go find the hard places. Does it hurt yet? Can you viscerally feel the pain from what you are hoping to make better?

Recently, the Stanford Graduate School of Business did some research, published in the *Journal of Positive Psychology*, in which they talked to nearly 400 people to learn whether people thought their lives were meaningful or happy.[5] They discovered a few related things:

- Satisfying your desires creates happiness, but it has nothing to do with a sense of meaning in life.
- Closer to the point, highly meaningful lives encounter lots of negative events and issues (hard places) that can cause reduced happiness.

• And about the end game—happiness is about getting what you want, meaningfulness is about expressing and defining yourself. A life of meaning is more deeply tied to a valued sense of self and one's purpose in life and community.

Being happy and living a life of meaning and purpose are not mutually exclusive. I'm just saying that creating real change, as in the cases of Eleuthera and Connie, may not always be about happiness. At times, it will be stressful and unhappy in the hard places of real change. Or as another friend, Paul Speer, told me "when given the choice of going down a path you know versus one you don't, pick the one you don't know. Because that puts you in uncomfortable and unfamiliar territory. . . . It's going to be an opportunity to do something that's really different with bigger impact." Paul also told me, in his community work, he feels like he "doesn't have time to not make an impact." More of that bad, sticky, double negative grammar.

It's about embracing that this social change work is hard, but in that experience, you are doing something of deep, meaningful purpose, what you are supposed to do. There are easier ways to do this and these regular heroes don't take that path. Going to the hard places creates a much deeper sense of identification and connection with what's really going on and with real people. And it will change *you*. There is deep purpose and profound meaning for the people willing to go there. As Amelia Earhart says:

> *The most difficult thing is the decision to act, the rest is merely tenacity. The fears are paper tigers. You can do anything you decide to do. You can act to change and control your life; and the procedure, the process is its own reward.*

Five Key Ideas from Chapter 3

1. If someone asked me what the most important question is of the seven, I might well say this one: Are you willing to go to the hard place? Answering it honestly and authentically takes some real thought and consideration and forces you to address some of the other six questions.

2. If you haven't yet felt some pain and hardship, you are almost certainly not close enough to the real problems to effect and be a part of real change.

3. Please spend some time thinking about what is meaningful versus what makes you happy. They aren't necessarily contradictory, but think about what will guide the direction you take.

4. What can you learn from your failures? Indeed, what *have* you learned from failures in your life that inform the pathway you want to take toward your *can't not do* in the future?

5. People have fears and insecurities about this work; that's completely okay. Know that you are not alone in feeling that way, this work of social change is hard and takes you out of your comfort zone if you really dig in.

PART II

How You Do This Work Well

CHAPTER 4

Jeff Tollefson, Losing It All and Becoming Richer

Are You Ready to Be Humble and Humbled?

Humility is the true key to success. Successful people lose their way at times.

They often embrace and overindulge from the fruits of success.

Humility halts this arrogance and self-indulging trap.

Humble people share the credit and wealth, remaining focused

and hungry to continue the journey of success.

    —Rick Pitino, basketball coach, University of Louisville

Jeff Tollefson was an investment banker and a successful one at that. He told me, "I allowed my feelings of self-worth to be so closely tied to how I was doing in my professional career and, of course, the measuring stick for so much of that was monetary reward and you get caught up in that. Then, all of a sudden after the market crashes, people are saying you aren't all that good, how could we miss the downturn? It was humbling and really forced me to step back and think about what it was that provides value in my life. I knew there had to be something deeper." He admits that he fell into that self-worth trap.

Jeff has a heart bigger than Minnesota. When I sit and talk with him, he has this constant air of forward-thinking optimism about him. He's an exceedingly likeable guy. You walk away from a conversation with Jeff rejuvenated and refreshed. Boy, I'd like to have more of what he has. Most people experiencing success and failure like Jeff's would fixate on the failure and get stuck in it, at least for a while. But Jeff used it as a springboard. Failure is going to happen; it's what we do next after we've fallen down, right?

Money isn't a good or bad thing. It doesn't have a soul. It doesn't have worth to us beyond economic. This isn't an anticapitalism diatribe; I spent my first 15 professional years in the private sector, and the wealth it generates is a key part of what makes philanthropy possible. Money is what we decide to make of it in our lives, consciously and sometimes unwittingly. When money starts to define our sense of who we are, then it becomes a big negative, a self-created one (that's a whole different book).

Jeff made a lot of money, then lost almost as much. It happens. But how many people will tell that story? How many of us can make what we *lost* and how we *failed* part of our personal story to share with the world? Jeff did. Think about it. Put yourself in his shoes. Would you be open and honest about how you far you had fallen? Not a lot of us would, but Jeff has.

"I was trying to figure out not what *could* I do, but what *should* I do next." Sounds like figuring out his can't not do. That's where Jeff was in 2007. He had made that familiar mistake of assuming his professional job and personal passion had to be separate and unconnected parts of his life. Sometimes that might be the case, but quite often one's profession and passion do not have to be mutually exclusive. Jeff told me, "I needed to find something that I was passionate about and, at the end of my time in managing our venture portfolios, I took the time to do it."

He left the firm and gave himself about six months to figure things out. He did a lot of reading of books by authors like Michael Josephson and Po Bronson. He also did a bit of nonconventional reading. "I had a lot of time to read the newspaper, and I got into reading obituaries and seeing what people had accomplished in their lives. I realized I had precious little to show for my first 45 years on this earth, so I set out to see what I could do in the second half on this planet that could be a little more significant," he explained.

Jeff also joined SVP Minnesota and started to learn what was going on in his community; in particular, he spent a lot of time with homeless youth. "I'd never met a teenager coming out of homelessness and when I did, it opened my eyes. . . . People talk about teaching people how to fish. These kids didn't even know fishing was a possibility."

He didn't expect a cause to find him, but one did, in part because his mind and heart were open. That kind of openness and humility go hand in hand. Without a mind open to possibility, humility strains to find room in our psyche. And without humility, it's unlikely our minds and hearts are truly open to what might be possible and unexpected.

One day in late 2007 in Minneapolis Jeff met a guy over lunch, who ran a Houston-based nonprofit called Genesys Works (www .genesysworks.org), aimed at helping at-risk teens. The organization places underprivileged high school students in meaningful internships with major corporations during their senior year in high school. They go through eight weeks of intensive technology training before they step into their internships. The guy's name was Rafael Alvarez, and he had been a corporate strategist for Hewlett-Packard before he became a regular hero.

"It was a week after my first conversation with him that I bought a ticket to fly down to Houston to learn more about the students," Jeff said. "Rafael told me about what his own life journey had been like and I began to visualize myself in his role and really doing something to help somebody else." Jeff flew home and started to develop the business plan for Genesys Works Twin Cities at his kitchen table.

He didn't see himself as the person to lead the agency. "My vision was to just hand off the baton to someone who could run the next leg of the relay, someone who really knew how to run a nonprofit." He kept rejecting the opportunity to lead Genesys Works Twin Cities, saying and thinking he wasn't the right person. This was coming from a successful businessperson whose specialty was creating, financing, and growing new businesses. He questioned his leadership skills on and off, but finally came to the realization "every time I thought things could be run by someone else I found myself pulling that baton back because I have never felt so fulfilled doing something." With an ample supply of his own humility, Jeff ultimately created the space to walk into at Genesys Works Twin Cities.

What kind of challenges did he encounter along the way to get Genesys Works going? Let's start with fear of failure. "I had convinced 16 high school juniors to dedicate their summer to an intensive professional skills training program with the reward being a paid year-long corporate internship when they were finished. The problem was that I didn't have enough jobs lined up at the beginning of the summer and didn't get the final commitments from companies until the last week of training. These young men and women had put their faith in me and I wasn't about to let them down. Words can't properly express how relieved and ecstatic I was when all the internship slots were finally secured. And as these students proved their worth in the workplace in the months that followed, they also validated our program model and we were off to the races. My fear of failure was ultimately replaced by complete confidence not only in what we were doing, but in the untapped potential of our urban youth." Just like Lisa Chin.

Once more from Jeff, "Most of my prior professional life was focused on trying to generate monetary gains for our investors and ultimately financial wealth for myself. But through my work at Genesys Works and my experiences with Social Venture Partners, I was able to redefine what wealth meant to me, and I soon realized that I was blessed with an abundance of riches far beyond what I ever thought possible. Not monetary wealth, but rich experiences and impactful relationships. I finally felt that I was living a life that matters; one not measured by financial success, but personal significance derived from the impact I knew I could have on the students I felt privileged to serve and the community in which I lived." Amen.

If it sounds like Jeff's story has threads of determined optimism and connected to one's core woven in, you'd be correct. What's fascinating is that Jeff's optimism and how connected this work is to his core might never have come to fruition without humility. If he can't admit his failures and be truly humbled, he never starts down this path. In his initial reluctance to take on the Genesys Works role, he left his ego out of it; he didn't try to fill the space until it was obvious he was the right guy. If arrogance or hubris is driving him, it clouds his thinking and closes his mind. And he likely never finds himself on this new path in life because he never opens up his mind and heart to "something he never felt so fulfilled doing." All of those threads of his experiences, grounded by his humility, came together into a life of deeper purpose.

What's the Point?

This is mostly about deeds not words. Words don't mean jack when it comes to the kind of authentic, powerful humility that makes change happen. I was listening to an interview the other day with someone on the radio, it doesn't matter who. He started off saying, "With all due respect . . . ," which meant that he was going to immediately disrespect someone or something, which he did. It's the same with humility. If someone goes out of their way to tell you they're humble, often they're not—at least not in the way that can be a powerful ingredient in helping people become more impactful in their change-the-world work.

Authentically humble people, regular heroes, have a sort of ego-less quality, a willingness to be vulnerable, to ask for help, to say, "I don't know." I'll call it humility on steroids and when you're around it, it stands out . . . or not. Another friend, like Larry Fox, who was an indispensable, inspiring partner for me in creating this book is Keith Kegley; he's a tech entrepreneur and engaged community member and a wonderful, creative thinker. When he was proofreading this chapter, he related to me that he worked once with a leader who began team meetings by sharing "what I don't want you to know about me is. . . . "

Keith told me that leader gets more from himself and his team when he's hiding nothing. And he's developed the muscle for being deeply authentic and vulnerable and it builds trust, respect, and a safe environment with the people he works with. It builds deep bonds of trust and loyalty. Humility in the form of authenticity and vulnerability is social glue, the glue that helps make real social change possible.

■ ■ ■

Elizabeth Svoboda, a science writer, published *What Makes a Hero? The Surprising Science of Selflessness.*[1] The words hero and selflessness together in the title speak volumes. It's a book about "how our genes compel us to do good for others and how acting generous can greatly improve your mental health. The book also reveals how we can encourage our most heroic selves to step forward."

Selflessness and humility are siblings. The core of Svoboda's research is from scientists and experts who believe we can each learn to build on our "natural biological endowments" and turn ourselves into models of selflessness and service for others. I'll drink to that and I'd like to drink more *of* that at times in my life. I can surely use more of it when I get drained or distracted. What I've experienced empirically are human traits that some scientists apparently believe can be turned on or off, if one just wants to learn how and invest the time. I like that.

Not only do you need to possess genuine and authentic humility, you also have to be willing to be humbled, to put your ego at risk and to be vulnerable. You have to know and embrace the fact that you are going to be put in uncomfortable positions, hard places, where you will not be in control. You may be called to task and you will have to own up to times when you are part of the problem, not the solution. This is not easy stuff. This work is neither for the fainthearted nor for the big egos that can't accept more than one dose of humility. If you don't get humbled more than once, you're probably still on the sidelines, not yet in the real game of hard, positive social change.

Power (and Humility?) in Philanthropy

It's pretty hard to overstate how important this humility thing is. It requires that you be exceptionally honest with yourself, looking in the mirror and truly examining your willingness to be humble in this work. This is particularly true if you are a "philanthropist," which is a word I dislike intensely, with its connotations of blue blood, class superiority.

Philanthropy connotes that you are a giver of your financial, as well as human, social and intellectual, capital to a social cause. If you define it that way, a philanthropist can be just about any engaged, concerned citizen who is willing to give of himself to help a fellow human being. When it comes to the money part, the relationship between a giver and receiver can be a beautiful thing when done well. Or it can be an ugly exercise in power and class. It is sometimes unintentional but it never gets called out or resolved because the nonprofit wants the resources so badly. Money can quickly become the 800-pound gorilla in the room.

Humility, or the lack of it, probably shows up more intensely and has more influence on outcomes in philanthropy than it does just about anywhere else in our lives. The success or failure of your giving, be it hundreds or millions of dollars, has so much to do with the humility with which you show up. That said, these lessons about power and humility go far beyond the realm of philanthropy. They can be applied to everything you do in your social change work. So as you read forward, don't assume this is only about philanthropy.

Social sector work is so often about bringing together people with resources, their own or an institution they represent, with people who need those resources to create positive change. As in any transaction in life, there are power and relationship dynamics that come into play when one party needs something from the other.

I've watched it play out time and time again. Often the one with the power doesn't even understand that her actions are creating problems. She isn't being humble, but she doesn't know it. It is subtle things, like the person who shows up at a nonprofit in his new BMW or talks about the fabulous new house he is building or how well his high-paying job is going. Sometimes the lack of humility is more explicit and intentional, as when a person gives a big gift with so many strings attached that it's hard to make the money even achieve its original goal. In either instance, these actions all convey a message of superiority. Trust and honesty have a hard time flourishing under these conditions; humility isn't even on the radar yet.

Money is an amplifier. If you were a grounded and humble person before you made some amount of money, chances are you'll be even more so with more money to invest in your community. Conversely, if you are full of ego and hubris or come at life with an "I have-it-you-need-it" mentality, your philanthropy will probably just amplify those bad characteristics. The chances of you finding out the truth, assuming you want to hear it, are small to none in philanthropic endeavors.

By "truth," I simply mean the messages your behavior conveys to the person receiving your gift. Arrogance or humility? Power or collegiality? Trust or control? I've watched both kinds of people time and time again and there are telltale signs of a lack of humility. These include:

- *How much control do you need to maintain over your gift?* I have a personal passion for this issue.[2] How many restrictions do you impose? There may be some minimal appropriate levels for large investments, but often what is expected is either wrong-headed or way out of proportion. This is perhaps the biggest barrier to more effective philanthropy. Let me explain it this way: If you're a successful businessperson, for example, you've had people or institutions invest funds in you at various stages. The restrictions are fairly straightforward—one party is giving the other party funds in expectation of a financial return at a later date. The investor may keep an eye on things or watch the financial results, but it's up to the company and its people to succeed or not. The investor would never tell the company what products to make, how to make them or to spend the money on product A but not product B, or only on research and development.

  There is usually no single bottom line, no one clear indicator of success, in the world of social change. Some philanthropists fill the void by creating their own indicators of success. The philanthropist will often tell the nonprofit that it can spend the money on X but not Y and that it can only spend Z percent on what the philanthropist considers to be overhead. Let's be clear. When I say restrictions, I don't mean mutual goals for social outcomes; I mean tying a nonprofit's hands by tightly restricting the specifics of how and where funds are spent. At SVP, we've learned this lesson over years of knowing that we have to trust the leadership to optimally spend the funds to build their organization and make hard decisions that are appropriate for them.[3]

Think about how impossible it would be to build a company if all of your funds came with such restrictions and if each separate investor had his or her own unique restrictions. Do the givers of resources believe the nonprofit can make the right decisions? Are the investors conveying the message that the nonprofit is the expert and knows the space better than they? Are they saying, "I trust you?" The answer is no to all of those if they overly restrict and control the funds. Yet, it's what happens all the time in the world of philanthropy. It's sometimes unintentional, perhaps unknown . . . but certainly not humble.

- *Do you ask anyone for feedback?* Do you ask independent-minded parties who have little to lose by giving you an honest perspective on your actions and behaviors? When you have some amount of money or power, who gives you honest feedback? The more you have of those two things, the less honest feedback you will hear from others around you, especially those you to whom you are giving that money. Let me repeat that. *The more money and power you have, the less honest feedback you will hear from others around you.* Humility requires you to be brutally honest with yourself, and when people are constantly telling you "thank-you, thank-you" and "you are really wonderful," it can get a little difficult to be humble.

  You better have a spouse, a sibling, a colleague, or a friend who will tell you the truth. Someone who will help you see your blind spots, where you have not been humble. Frankly, some people may not want that feedback, they just want to believe their own story. But if you want to be the kind of person who creates real lasting change, who can inspire others and lead a movement, humility will be one of the most powerful assets you can bring to the table.

- *Are you imposing your vision on the recipient or are you investing in their vision?* It's certainly good to have your own vision, but is that vision backed with a deep knowledge of the cause, the players, and the current work in the field? Some of you will remember Tom Peters' famous expression "stick to your knitting."[4] What he meant, very simply, is to stick to what you know and, just as importantly, keep your nose out of places where you don't know what you're talking about or don't do so until you've taken the time to listen and learn a lot.

If you write down a list of things you know a lot about, I would bet that helping at-risk kids or changing environmental policy or other social causes, is probably not on that list for most of us. If you give resources to an organization doing that work, don't tell them how to run their programs. Let them be the experts or don't invest in them in the first place. You need to find an organization that shares your vision, not one that you can bend to your will. Figure out which experts you believe in and invest in them. Let them do what they do and stay out of their way. You should want account-ability, but focus it on the social end goals of their work, like academic success or forest health, not things like how much they spend on the copier.

- *How close are you willing to get to the real, on-the-street, difficult work (hard places) to better understand the challenges and effects of your contribution firsthand?* Simply put, have you ever felt uncomfortable, out of place, scared, or worried in the course of your philanthropy? If it has felt all good with no rough spots, then you haven't truly gotten involved. You haven't dug in enough to know where the problems really are and how hard they are to solve. You almost certainly haven't been truly humble or humbled yet. Yes, you should celebrate progress, but you have to find the challenge, the hard work if you want to create real change in the world . . . and in yourself. If you want to change both, the pathway will ultimately take you to places of humility and being humbled.

Humility Has Power

Kevin Shaw was fortunate, maybe savvy, enough to make about as much as Jeff lost. He's an entrepreneur who built and sold a company in Cleveland, Ohio. He fits in his social change work today part-time alongside a new business in which he is working. He joined SVP Cleveland in 2003 and was heavily involved with one of the non-profits in which that group invested. He is one of those people you can just feel has a good soul, if you know what I mean. The guy couldn't fake it if he had to, and he cares deeply about other people in a palpable, visceral way. In every conversation I have with Kevin he always listens before he talks, considers all sides of an issue, and is constantly open to a new way of thinking about things. People just like being around him.

Jeff and Kevin are both equally committed to and effective in their community work. When you talk to Kevin about causes he cares about, some of the first things he'll tell you are "I want to see how much I can contribute and learn," and "I know I haven't done enough, I've only taken baby steps," and "it's not clear to me yet where my strongest passions lie, I'm still figuring it out."

The word humility doesn't show up anywhere in his explanation and he doesn't have to say it. Be truly honest with yourself. Do Kevin's statements resonate with you or do you think you have things figured out? Are you in learning mode or an I-have-the-answer mindset? One of the most powerful things about talking with Kevin is how strongly he sees this work as a learning journey. His mind is open and receptive and humble. He is not driven by ego. In a 23-minute interview with him, I went back and counted how many times he used the word "learn," or some derivative of it: 14 times.

To Kevin, the work is never done; we all need to do more and the first place to look is at ourselves. Asking yourself for more money, effort, and sweat equity before you ask anyone else to give more is powerful. When someone we work with is hardest on himself, we want to work harder and help that other person more. When you are the kind of person who is always asking questions, not pushing your answers on everyone first, you inspire others to be more inquisitive, less assumptive. And when you live your life like you are on an authentic journey, people want to come alongside to help you, work with you, and share the load with you.

Kevin shows why humility can be so powerful in a group, in a meeting, in a movement:

- There is a positive power and energy that is created with people like Kevin in the room. There is "more oxygen in the room."
- The energy and work is all about the real problems and working on solutions, not about balancing egos and personal agendas. No wasted time or energy.
- True humility that you find in people like Kevin eventually attracts more and more people with that attitude. Pretty soon, you have a room, maybe even a movement, full of truly committed people who make real change happen. Or the converse, the arrogant person drives people out of the room over time.

Like the saying goes, it's amazing how much can get done when no one cares who gets the credit.

■ ■ ■

A friend, Tony, who is a regional VP of a national contractor, provides a quick example of the power of humility. I was in a seminar with him one day, the general topic was leadership and how leaders show up authentically with their people. The consultant working with the group that day veered the discussion toward this willingness to be vulnerable (thanks, Brene Brown[5]), and Tony asked what the heck vulnerability had to do with leadership. We'd talked about honesty, but where does vulnerability fit in to the leader equation? The consultant spelled it out exactly like this: *honesty + vulnerability = humility*. People want to follow, are almost desperate for, a leader like that.

Just in case you start to think this humble(d) stuff just applies to social change work, where we all have to get along, listen to Laszlo Bock, the guy in charge of hiring these days at Google. To him, there are five key hiring attributes, one of which is humility. Bock says: "feeling the sense of responsibility . . . to try to solve the problem, and the humility to step back and embrace the better ideas of others . . . what we can do together is problem solve. I've contributed my piece, and then I step back." He goes on, "it's not just humility in creating space for others to contribute, it's intellectual humility. Without humility, you are unable to learn."[6]

Your Mindset

I don't remember the guy's name, but I can still see the CBS News story like it was yesterday, even though it was about 15 years ago. It was about someone who had made a bunch of money working at Microsoft in the 80s and 90s and now he was driving race cars. The interviewer asked him why he thought he'd made enough money to be able to retire and race cars when he was 40. His answer was short, emphatic, and crystal clear in his mind. "Because I worked for it. I worked so hard all those years, I've earned this." I still shake my head even as I write it down. How can anyone believe they worked hard enough to make a hundred times more money than the next person? It speaks for itself.

Do you think the money you have made is 100 percent because you earned it with your hard work, that you worked harder and smarter than anyone else, and that you deserve it all? There is usually some degree of truth in there, but this is more about your mindset. Do you come from a place of gratitude and a feeling of good fortune? Do you recognize the ways in which you didn't just work harder, but you were lucky because of where you grew up or who you happened to meet one day or because you could afford the education that gave you access to particular networks of people?

It's hard to overstate how meaningful this "I deserve it" versus "I was lucky" mindset about money and power is. The reality of the answer doesn't matter nearly as much as the perception, the true lens through which a person sees the world. If you feel you are mostly lucky (and yes, you worked hard, too), you are more likely to have an open mind, a giving heart, a happier soul and life. If you feel you deserve what you have, you will be more closed off to potential, more likely to hoard your money and power, and often lead a less happy, even tragic, life. That isn't hyperbole. I've watched money and power in the right hands do such good for the world. And, I've watched it, in the wrong hands or being mishandled, destroy relationships, families, and lives.

Level 5 Leaders and Humility

Many of you are familiar with Jim Collins, maybe the most insightful and followed leadership guru of the past 20 years. He is the author of the iconic book on building the highest-performing companies, *Good to Great*. He also wrote a shorter piece titled, *Good to Great and the Social Sector*.[7] The question Collins started out asking was, "Can a good company become a great company and, if so, how?" These are the biggest companies in the world that have broken the curve and sustained exceptional, far-above-the-norm financial performance for 20-plus years—in other words, it wasn't just random success. Collins argues that one of the key ingredients that allows a company to become great is having a Level 5 Leader, which he defines as an executive in whom genuine personal *humility* blends with intense professional *will*. Does intense will sound akin to determined optimism?!

That's pretty amazing when you think about it. He didn't isolate brains, particular experiences, or upbringing but instead empirically discovered the two most powerful traits of exceptional leaders, one of which is genuine personal humility. One of the most likely and significant Level 5 Leaders in history was, in Collins' opinion, Abraham Lincoln.

I just happened to pick up that book again a few weekends ago and do some reading for another project I was working on and the Level 5 Leader just jumped off the page at me. Some of the defining characteristics include never boastful (humble), calm determination (determined optimism), and firm resolve no matter how difficult (hard places). I can probably quit here trying to make the case for humility as a key lever in your tool kit for being more effective at your can't not do; Collins already did it many years ago.

Collins also recently penned a piece for *Inc. Magazine* about time he spent teaching at West Point, and much of what he wrote about was the relationship of the cadets to failure, that is, to being humbled.[8] Collins said he found something very unique, "They've put themselves in an environment where you can't go through *without* failing." Indeed repeated failure is built into the culture, yet it didn't faze the cadets in the least; they came across as "irrepressibly positive and devoid of the alienation that afflicted other college campuses" where Collins has taught. Why? One cadet told him simply, "success is not the primary point. I go back, to places where I've failed, because it's making me better. It is making me stronger. If I am not failing, I am not growing." The same is true and possible for anyone willing to wade into social change work and be humbled. You will grow and be stronger.

Collins concluded, "It is very difficult to have a great life unless it is a meaningful life. And it is very difficult to have a meaningful life without meaningful work. . . . The cadets in my seminars have been some of the happiest, most engaged, and most purposeful young men and women I've ever met."

My Own Lesson in Humility

For me, humility is a core value in my life. I'd like to think I exhibit some of it in how I work and live. But a colleague bluntly told me a while ago, "Shoemaker, sometimes your humility is just bullshit."

I deeply value Nancy's insights so I was shocked when she told me that in the middle of a coaching session. She was basically telling me that I was using my humility as a cover, a mask to hide behind at times. Why did I do this? Because sometimes it's easier, it's less trouble, and it keeps me from rocking the boat. Of course, I could convince myself that I held back because of my humility. Just like there are good and bad forms of optimism, there are good and bad forms of humility.

When Nancy told me that, it sort of threw me back on my heels. I thought, "Oh really, Nancy, and who made you the expert? I can tell you a lot of people who would disagree with you." But the more I thought about it, the more I realized she was right. I was telling myself an internal story about my humility, and then I sometimes use it to shy away from owning my role in the community.

I share this to emphasize how hard genuine, authentic humility is. And how hard it is to live it. If you asked a lot of people if I'm a humble person, my guess is a lot of them would say, "Yes, of course," and that would feel good. What doesn't feel good is Nancy making me see a truth. Humility in the name of only doing so much or worrying about offending someone when the truth will have greater impact is not much better than arrogance. Which is worse? Saying something that's wrong and uninformed or not saying something that you know is right and grounded because you don't want to offend someone?

Genuine humility is about constantly learning. It's not about holding back and saying you don't know anything. It's about listening and asking questions more often than talking and giving answers. It's not about being silent when the truth needs to be said. All of us have a positive power we can bring to our community work. The balancing act between using that power humbly versus being arrogant is a tricky one.

Let me describe that balancing act from one more angle, again tapping into my friend, Keith's wisdom. He reminded me that "yesterday's humble pie can easily become tomorrow's ego trip. When we learn that humility is social currency it can be almost natural to then use that currency again and again to get people to like and go along with us. You have to be constantly aware of this pitfall and hold yourself to extreme humility or humility on steroids. You'll have to rediscover your humility over and over again, aware that your ego wants to use, and maybe abuse, the currency that works."

Even the Great Are Humbled

One of my favorite figures in history is Winston Churchill. The thing that fascinates me most about him, beyond his speeches and his intellectual range, is how many times he failed, was truly humbled, and then came back again.

His military disaster at Gallipoli in 1915 and the lives it cost are infamous, but he came back to be one of the great wartime leaders of history. He was a political failure in the 1930s only to be beckoned back to save Britain and Europe in the 1940s. Soon after winning World War II, he lost again politically only to resurrect himself once more through his writings as a prolific author. Churchill was not a humble man, but he was humbled time and time again, and he didn't let it stop him.

What's the value of being humbled? We're not fighting world wars in this social change work, but we are fighting wars against crime, poverty, weak leadership, homelessness, and all the entrenched environmental and social challenges. We need to be ready to be humbled if we are going to win. I hope that this chapter will empower the bashful to use their humility to grow as powerful leaders and help the brash become more self-aware of their arrogance. And I hope it will help both groups to understand the fulfillment and real power that can come from their humility. When we get humbled, really knocked back on our heels, it means we've gotten close enough to the real problem to truly learn what matters, to feel the problem enough that it hurts, and to show our authentic commitment to the cause. We have been humble and humbled.

Five Key Ideas from Chapter 4

1. Humility makes a lot of answers to other questions more possible, because you are more open and less guarded about what answers you might find regarding what you are a determined optimist about, and who you are at your core.
2. Sort of like working in the hard places, if you haven't yet been humbled in this work, you probably aren't deep enough yet, not clear enough yet about your can't not do. You're still too much on the surface.
3. Humility attracts other people; it's contagious in a different way than optimism, but just as powerfully.
4. Money is an amplifier and whatever humility, or lack thereof, that you already possess, money will serve to increase.
5. Humility is a tricky balancing act; being too silent is sometimes no better than being too loud or arrogant.

CHAPTER 5

Lori, I Got Married a Little Too Early to the *Right* Woman

Can You Actively Listen?

> *Most people do not listen with the intent to understand; they listen with the intent to reply.*
> — Stephen R. Covey, *The 7 Habits of Highly Effective People*[1]

Habit 5: Seek First to Understand, Then to Be Understood

My wife, Lori, has this incredible gift. It comes very naturally to her, just second nature, she was born with it. She is an incredible listener. Your first reaction to that might be "that's so nice, she must be so sweet" or something to that effect. Nope, you'd be missing the point. I think everyone can relate to that occasional experience when we meet or sit with someone who is a great listener, and I mean a truly, authentically deep listener. It is an empowering experience. You feel heard. You feel your own sense of personal power after spending time with a great listener. It's just one of the many reasons I am so madly in love with this woman after more than 30 years.

We got married when we were 21, which is kind of hard. You're just not a fully formed adult yet; I'm still working on it. But there were some things that just drew me inexorably toward her, and one of her beautiful traits was her ability to fully, authentically listen. A few months ago, we were driving around on a Saturday afternoon, running errands, and I asked Lori why she listens the way she does, what's her mindset? She gave me this matter of fact response: "because I want to hear and understand the other person." I pushed a little more and she said "because I want to hear and understand the other person."

I finally got a little more out of her. "Whenever someone says something, there is a subtext or a nuance to it and unless I am fully listening, especially face to face, I'll miss it." So it's about a lot more than just the words that are spoken. Yep, that makes sense. She didn't say this part, but I think the depth of her listening is what also unlocks reciprocity. She's taken it on herself to listen as deeply as she has so that she can count on the reciprocity that she really values. And she knows, intuitively, she can create that reciprocity by the way she listens first. A less skilled listener might listen with the expectation of reciprocity but not understand her role in encouraging that. I knew I made the right decision to ask her to marry me, even if it was a little too early; thankfully, she agreed.

In case you're wondering, listening is one of my many challenges and it starts right where this chapter starts, with Lori at home. I am not even one-tenth the listener that she is. Dang it, I am always working at it, trying to get better. I have stretches of hours when I really listen to her well. I pay attention to any time my mind drifts. I look at her intently and listen fully. But then, I falter and I don't listen well for five minutes or five seconds and completely miss something. It can just kill the trust and energy built over the last few hours. It's no different with the people we are working with to create change in the world (or in our companies, for that matter).

What's the Point?

Being a great listener is one of the most powerful skills a person can possess. That does not mean, by the way, that our world values it; we don't nearly enough. The ability to listen deeply will give you more power to do good than almost any other attribute you could possess. This is not a touchy-feely psychology lesson; this is about being an effective leader for change, plain and simple. It is a skill that can be learned. Or maybe you're like Lori and you were just born with the gift. Most of us really don't listen very well. Maybe we listen a bit, but we are usually just waiting until the other person finishes so we can get our two cents into the conversation.

When I talk about listening, I don't mean just with your ears. It's about your mindset, your whole approach. In a piece for *Time* magazine, Annie Murphy Paul, author of *Brilliant: The New Science of Smart*, affirms that "effective listening involves more than simply hearing the words that float past our ears. Rather, it's an active process of interpreting information and making meaning." She continues, "Though listening is often treated as a social nicety, it's also one of the most powerful tools we have to gain information and insight."[2]

Do you study, absorb, understand, try to get the whole situation and all its complexity and nuances? You can't make the gray world of social progress black and white, you just can't. When you actively listen, you can hear, feel, and see all the gray. You have to; you can't not. A friend of mine uses the expression "listen for the music, not just the words," to convey the notion of listening fully and deeply.

A first cousin of listening is asking questions. Ask questions before telling answers. Heck, it's why I structured this book the way I did, inviting you into questions. Listening is not just about your ears and hearing. It's about the way you bring your whole self to the table of social change.

In a fairly well-known piece of research about how we convey messages and feelings to someone else, Albert Mehrabian concluded that the quality of the message conveyed is determined only 7 percent by the words used, with the remaining 93 percent based on nonverbal cues such as facial expressions and body language.[3] In the same way, listening is only in small proportion a result of hearing the specific words said and much more about striving to grasp the intent and feeling.

■   ■   ■

Ernesto Sirolli has worked all over the world in the field of economic development. His TEDx talk on the importance of listening is informative and funny.[4] He talks about the comedy of errors that he experienced when he and a group of like-minded Italians went to Africa to help a small village learn to plant crops. It was a good news/ bad news story. The good news? Their crops of zucchini and tomatoes flourished in the hot climate. The bad news? Before they could harvest the food, an army of hippopotami devoured everything one morning. Years later, he can laugh when he says, "Instead of asking them why they were not growing anything, we simply said, 'Thank God, we're here.'" They *told* before they *listened*. When you fully and authentically listen, before telling, a bunch of awesome things happen:

- *The person you are actively listening to becomes much more powerful in positive ways.* When you listen to someone describe a challenge or a solution, you allow her to think through the challenges, possible solutions, and outcomes. You help him see that so much more is possible because he described it himself. Oftentimes, people can figure out solutions by listening to themselves out loud. This is no more complex than the age-old "teach them how to fish versus fish for them" story. If we listen long and deeply enough, someone else in the room, that person sitting across from us, may well know the answer, and when he brings it out for himself, he owns the solution and the future, not you. You can get on to the next problem because someone owns the one you were just trying to solve; she can fish for herself.

• *Just as powerfully, the people that you listen to become your trusted allies over time.* This trust stuff takes time but, besides good ol' honesty, nothing builds trust better and more deeply than listening. Just think about what that means for creating positive change. You create powerful people who have a greater vision for what is possible and, at the same time, you also build more trust in your relationships.

• *You talk less and your words have greater impact.* God gave you two ears and one mouth for a reason, right? Then, when you *do* talk, people listen—a *lot* more. My first boss at Microsoft, Dawn Trudeau, is another great listener. In meetings, she doesn't say a lot. If you're wondering whether that's because she is shy or a shrinking violet, stop. She can kick butt, when needed, with the best of 'em. I've watched her in meetings, taking notes, listening, taking more notes, pondering, thinking. After almost everyone else has practically broken their necks stretching to have every single thought in their heads uttered out loud, Dawn will say a few powerful and pointed sentences.

Yes, Dawn is smart so what she says has value because of her brain, but it's also the way she does it that makes her words so powerful. When she talks, everyone in the room listens intently. You can literally see people lean forward. If you remember the old E.F. Hutton commercials, "When E.F. Hutton talks, people listen," that's Dawn. She is the most effective and powerful person in the room because she says less and listens more than anyone else.

How does all of this add up to making you a more effective leader for social change? Every time you listen deeply and authentically, you do a little more to create another leader for the cause. You help other people understand their personal power—and you're not just creating more leaders but more *effective* leaders around you. You engender a level of trust and build relationships with the people around you that will serve you through the hard times, which are surely part of the journey to create positive change. And you become more powerful, in every good sense of the word, because your words count for more and you've empowered more and more people. More leaders, power, and trust, is that enough for starters?

There is so much good inside each of us just waiting to be unleashed, and there is no more effective valve to release all that good than a great listener. Think about the opposite experience of talking with a person who will not stop talking about herself and what she cares about. People like this rarely, if ever, listen. Do you feel compelled to work with or for them? Best case, we all walk away rolling our eyes or just think that was a zero-sum experience. More likely, depending on how much of a big mouth we just spent time with, we end up feeling drained, less optimistic, more ready to just finish working and go home where we can relax and block out the day. This listening stuff matters in our day-to-day lives, of course, it's just that it matters so much more in this change-the-world work.

Levels of Listening, Where Are You?

Mike Myatt is a leadership adviser to Fortune 500 CEOs and boards and author of *Hacking Leadership*.[5] He says, "The big miss for most leaders is that they fail to understand that the purpose of communication is not to message, but to engage. . . . It's about focusing on understanding the needs of others." That means listening. The engagement Myatt speaks of is an art, accessed by listening. Engagement can be measured by the depth of listening you draw out of others and the level of passion they activate with. The better your skill at listening the deeper the engagement you can access. According to

Myatt, there are four different types of listeners. Be honest with yourself, which kind of listener are you?

1. The *nonlistener* is concerned with doing most of the talking, constantly interrupting the speaker, rarely interested in what the speaker has to say, and usually has the last word.
2. The *marginal listener* hears the sounds and some of the words but does not really listen. It is superficial listening. The listener stays on the surface of a problem, never going deeper.
3. The *evaluative listener* is actively trying to hear what the speaker is saying, but isn't making enough effort to understand the intent. Evaluative listeners form opinions about the speaker's words before the message is complete and miss part of the true meaning of the message.
4. The *active listener* refrains from evaluating the speaker's words and attempts to see things from the speaker's point of view. Active listeners listen not only for content but for the intent and feeling behind the message, as well. They are usually skillful questioners, too; they hear the words, not just the music. That's Lori.

This is a Fortune 500 management consultant talking about listening and leaders. If you are a marginal listener today, maybe you can make evaluative your goal for this next year, and then move up. Becoming an active listener is where real power to be a change leader lies. It is through active listening that you create trusted allies and empowered people.

You Hear Interesting Things When You Listen

Ben Franklin said, "Speak little, do much." It is hard to do. Almost everyone with whom I spoke for this book, and who you are reading about on these pages, has admitted that becoming a better listener was something they had to change about themselves, sometimes a little, sometimes a lot, and everyone is constantly working on it. I told you a little about Bill Henningsgaard in the introduction. When I first met Bill (Dawn's cousin, by the way), he was a vice president of sales. He wasn't a particularly bombastic guy in his earlier professional career, but I do remember being in meetings where he was, like the rest of us, mainly focused on getting his point across. Why wouldn't he be? We all figured that was the best, fastest route to impressing our bosses and influencing others. That might be true for that one meeting for the short-term but not for the long-term.

Fast forward a few years. The Henningsgaard family has a long-standing commitment to civic engagement. Over time, Bill began to immerse himself in local social issues. In 2010, he happened to be sitting in a small chair in the local public school's library listening to a presentation and thinking about how much money he was going to get asked to donate. He was half listening to the presenter until a few grim statistics about the school's population—70 percent of kids qualify for free and reduced lunch, up from 50 percent only a few years before—made him pay closer attention.

He said, "All of a sudden, I found myself listening with a different set of ears." This school was three miles from Microsoft's sprawling campus and one mile from his kids' public school. It is an affluent area, generally. Bill told me, "I'd considered myself well-educated and engaged, but had missed the change in our community." He didn't just hear what was being said; he listened. And he didn't just listen to the words, he absorbed the meaning and a larger purpose that went far beyond that room.

What he heard jolted him into action, much like Jeff Tollefson had been after he talked with some homeless teens and Kerry McLenehan when she heard the facts about kindergarteners in her community. In one short year, Bill was helping lead Eastside Pathways (www.eastsidepathways.org), a bold, communitywide initiative to organize resources to "support every child, step by step, from cradle to career, in his/her community." The organization is all about bringing the right people together to create change across the community. Basically, everyone involved in the community has to give a little to get a lot, the proverbial whole being greater than the sum of its parts. Managing this huge pool of resources takes a unique form of leadership. Most likely someone who knows all the answers, tells everyone those answers, and then keeps telling everyone what to do, right? Not even close.

Bill told me that he eventually learned that one of the most powerful things he could do was make sure the right people were in the room, be a connector, and then shut up for as long as he could. I remember him telling me about one meeting where he realized he just had to make sure the right four or five people, who had never been well connected before the meeting, were in the room. His role was to "listen intently for the gaps and holes that I could help fill." That expression reminds me of building a campfire; sometimes it's the space, the oxygen between the logs that makes a fire burn brighter, not piling on more logs. The real goal of the meeting that day was to make sure relationships "burned brighter" between the people in the room and not for Bill to pile on more of what he had to say. And the best way for him to ensure all that was to actively listen.

He knew that the people in the room knew the answers; they just needed to be convened and connected and listened to. And they needed to listen to each other. Who said the least and listened the most? Bill. Who was the most powerful person in that room? Often Bill, just like Dawn. Damn, it's just not possible to describe how much we all miss him sometimes.

It's the difference between position power and referent power that I remember from my Management 101 books. With the former, you are the leader and people follow because they *have* to; with the latter, you are the leader and more people follow because they *want* to. Which form of power do you think is more effective, sustainable, and replicable? In this community work, referent carries the day.

Let me reiterate, I'm not talking about listening as a nice, polite thing to do. There is more creativity and potential unleashed in the room when there are more great listeners. The same is true of any organization—be it in the private or public sector. I've just been watching it for the past 17 years in the nonprofit sector. This work is not about you winning the meeting; this is about you helping change the world. That is the ultimate victory.

■ ■ ■

A while back, when I was trying to learn how listening might tangibly affect my ability to lead, I wondered if there was any research or scientific basis for the beliefs I'm sharing here. It took a little digging, but sure enough in the February 2012 issue of the *Journal of Research in Personality* is an article titled "The Role of Listening in Interpersonal Influence."[6] Bingo! The authors explain that what they found, in rigorous testing, was that that "listening = power" for at least two reasons. First, you gain more access to others' beliefs, knowledge, and attitudes, in part because people disclose information more readily. Second, listening also enables you to tailor your persuasive behavior to that particular context. In sum, those who listen reap both informational and relational benefits that make them more influential."

The game I try to play with myself in meetings is jotting down my thoughts in the margin of a piece of paper and then waiting to see if someone else says that same thing. If they do, I'm good; it's been said and I can cross it off. If they don't, then eventually I'll speak up. I am very aware of how much more effective the whole room is when I shut up, especially when I'm in the formal leadership role. Yes, there is a time to talk, when a leadership voice needs to be heard. Just be intentional about it. Save it up like a precious asset. Your leadership ears can be just as powerful, often more powerful, than your leadership voice. I need to remind myself of that all the time.

Five Key Ideas from Chapter 5

1. Active listening can be learned and almost everyone has something to learn about listening more effectively.
2. This is not just about your ears, but your whole approach and mindset regarding leading, working with people, and creating change in the world.
3. The people you listen to effectively become more powerful and will be your allies for the future. You just get a lot more done.
4. Hearing someone else talk, but not working to understand the full, real intent of what she is saying is not enough. You need to be able to listen for the intent and feeling of the person you are listening to.
5. Asking great questions is the natural companion to active, effective listening.

CHAPTER 6

Suzi Levine, Learning When Not to Raise Her Hand

Do You Believe 1 + 1 = 3?

The whole is greater than the sum of its parts.

—Aristotle

"I've always been an individual contributor. Somebody who can power through things really well on my own." When she was growing up, "you name the club, I was in it, and I became the president of it." Suzi Levine, who you met in the prologue, is a master connector today, but she didn't start out that way, as her words above convey. Like many of the skills these regular heroes have developed over the years, learning to believe in the power of building connections is a slow, and sometimes arduous, process. We need people who step up like she did, no doubt, but she might not have always had enough of the right people coming along for the ride.

During the summer between her freshman and sophomore years of college, Suzi traveled by herself through Europe for six weeks.

As she told me, "I had the opportunity to have a lot of conversations with myself. Then I went to Israel in the fall and one of the biggest lessons I learned was what 'community' means. It is where people open their homes, where people care about each other, where it is completely nonjudgmental."

It was in this context that she started to develop some of the skills that have made her a great connector today. She continued, "I learned to ask questions. I learned to ask the dumbest questions. I learned to formulate better questions. And then, I learned the value of having better questions than having answers." That was a very different Suzi from the young woman at the end of her freshman year.

Over time, Suzi changed. She had to. It started in college, with the train rides in Europe and trip to Israel and it continued through life. Between having two kids, a personal financial crisis, and being part of the Jewish community where she lives, she eventually realized that "getting where I wanted to go," in other words, meeting her future goals for her community, was about empowering others and recognizing the superpowers that different people have. "It's more about listening. It's about active listening [her words, not mine]. I think I was always so concerned with people thinking that I was smart and raising my hand." How many of us can relate? And how many of us have the guts, the wisdom, the self-awareness to eventually come to realize that it's not about people thinking we are smart but instead about empowering and connecting?

To bring it full circle, she says, "now I like putting puzzle pieces together. You remember James Burk, the science historian, who used to connect seemingly unrelated items? For example, he'd say something like, 'Let me show you how this hot dog is connected to this light bulb [not really, but I get the point, Suzi], that's me. I love making connections between things. And being the listener, it's only by listening and asking questions that you can be a great connector." Suzi is one of those friends that I wish everyone could meet, because I know you'd like her. After getting to know her over the years, I have no doubt that learning to be a connector was something that eventually became more natural for her, but she did have to learn how to not always lead from the front.

■ ■ ■

Let's pick up some more of Suzi's story, where we left off in the introduction, back in 2005 in that old building on the south edge of the campus of the University of Washington, where two leading researchers, Pat Kuhl and Andy Meltzoff, were doing world-class brain research, truly cutting edge, at the Institute for Learning & Brain Sciences (I-LABS, http://ilabs.washington.edu). Pat and Andy not only knew the facts, they were fundamentally optimistic that their findings could change the lives of millions of newborns and young children. Along with another colleague, they published their research in *The Scientist in the Crib: What Early Learning Tells Us about the Mind.*[1] As I said up front, their work was not yet reaching far enough beyond the hallways and conferences of their fellow academics, and most surely, not into the living rooms of enough parents of young, growing children.

But it did reach one parent—Suzi. At the time, Suzi was part of an SVP grant committee that was exploring grant opportunities in early childhood education. Often these grant committees will seek out experts to help inform their efforts to find effective nonprofits to work with. Suzi brought the group to I-LABS and the committee began to focus on the work of I-LABS itself. It turns out that another member of that grant committee was Bill Henningsgaard. So this put two master connectors in the same room, with two determined optimists, Pat and Andy.

The group's visit to the lab was illustrative. They asked a lot of questions and listened intently for the import and the potential of the work Pat and Andy were doing. At one point they asked what I-LABS could do if it wasn't limited by resources. What would they do if they could go as far as they dreamed? This ignited Suzi's can't not do.

Suzi and Bill came away from the meeting determined to help I-LABS fulfill its dreams. A meeting a few days later helped everyone codify a direction. After that, Suzi and Bill helped them compose a strategic plan and the first call to action was the creation of an advisory board. The connectors started connecting with other connectors. They tapped their networks to create a new board and worked together to develop strategies to raise I-LABS' profile. When they realized they would need more resources, they did more connecting. Big missing pieces filled in. Just two years later, on May 24, 2007, Suzi, Bill, Andy, and Pat were able to celebrate a new world-class brain-imaging facility. The governor, university president, local and regional civic and business leaders, the media, and more were there. Today, presidents and Nobel researchers look to I-LABS as a world leader in early childhood brain research.

I was, proudly, one of the connectors who helped put a few of the I-LABS pieces together[2] and I will never forget the feeling of that May 24th gathering. It was a beautiful spring evening on a gorgeous college campus. I walked in and started looking at some of the exhibits they'd set up for this celebration; they were cool. But what struck me far more profoundly, and I can still vividly remember the feeling to this day, was walking around and seeing someone I knew I'd played a role in getting involved . . . then another person . . . and another person. It was sort of like walking around seeing different pieces of the completed puzzle. I remembered each of them individually, but it wasn't until May 24th that I saw all of the pieces come together and felt the cumulative effect of all the individual connections. It was such a powerful, humbling lesson about the value of connecting the right people even though, at the time, I didn't always know what would end up happening. In this case, it was something beautiful to behold. Their work will affect the lives of millions of newborns in the future.

What's the Point?

Why does connection matter? Why is it so key to making things work? What value does it create when it comes to empowering people to solve social challenges? Nothing here is rocket science and yet, we often don't value it nearly enough. Let me give you three short, emblematic examples that elucidate the incremental, significant, sometimes game-changing value that results from being a connector.

1. An ant colony is an organized and productive system. No individual ant ever sees the whole system, yet the contribution of each ant is critical and each, in turn, benefits from the greater whole they collectively create. There are people who study ant colonies in great detail. Why? Because people like Deborah Gordon, at Stanford's Biological Sciences Department, are "interested in systems where individuals unable to assess the global situation still work together in a coordinated way, i.e. the parts create a whole greater than the sum of the parts."[3] Connections create much more potential than people and parts do individually. *More potential.*

2. Meg Wheatley, who studies organizational behavior, has said, "Who we become together will always be different than who we were alone. . . . When living beings link together, they form systems that create more possibilities." She goes on, "We discover we are not alone. There is no power equal to a community discovering what it cares about. Real change begins with the simple act of people talking about what they care about. It takes two or three people to notice they're concerned about the same thing and then the world begins to change. . . . Friends talk to friends. They talk to others and it grows and grows."[4] Connecting empowers and emboldens us because we know we are not alone. *More possibilities.*

3. Metcalfe's Law[5] says that as the number of nodes in a network increases arithmetically, the value of the network increases exponentially. Or as Kevin Kelley explained many years ago in *New Rules for the New Economy*[6] if four people join a network, there are six potential one-to-one connections. If you add a fifth, the network increases to 10 connections, and so on. Kelley explains,

"Each additional member increases the network's value, which, in turn, attracts more members, initiating a spiral of benefits. . . . A connected object in a network that interacts in some way with other nodes, can give birth to a hundred unique relationships that it could never do while unconnected." Connections make things possible that weren't possible and creates new things that didn't exist. *More relationships.*

More potential, possibilities, and relationships. Just like humility and listening, I want you to know that connecting isn't just a nice-to-have, it's a strategic-level imperative in making real change happen.

1 + 1 = 3 with Connectors

Bill Henningsgaard told me a few more things, actually a lot more things, over the years, that really struck me, "I've always been motivated by this opportunity to make 1 + 1 = 3 instead of 2. All these individual organizations are working their butts off to try to get something done, and I always try to find the connection that adds value somewhere. . . . The absence of something like Eastside Pathways would mean some of these one-off opportunities [individual organizations doing good, but isolated, work] show up for a little bit, but sometimes go away. . . . There is a constant existence of the opportunity to connect unconnected efforts."

All of those statements represent a relentlessly open system view of the world. You have to be a connector of the parts and people as much and as often as you can. You have to use your eyes and ears at the right times to create those connections. You can't just own or solve these challenges by yourself. I am not talking about your traditional, built-in social or work circles. This is being motivated, even hungry, to connect people even when they don't look, act, or behave like you. It's impossible to overstate how important the principles are here. You cannot change the world without human connection.

You can say this is sort of obvious, and it may be. But, how often do each of us really do it? How much connecting do you do? I can almost guarantee the answer is not enough, at least not yet. When you walk into a meeting, are you looking around to see who isn't there who should be? Do you always follow up with people to make sure the dots or people get connected? Do you keep track of who you've contacted and when you should contact them next and connect them to someone else? You need your tribe, but we'll get to Seth Godin in a minute.

The ideas in this chapter are as foundational as any in the whole book. I've been involved in building SVP in 39 cities in eight countries these past 17 years; we've engaged over 4,000 SVP partners and worked with over 300 nonprofits. What I've learned is that the solutions exist, the money and resources often exist. But what we lack most is enough connected human capital—people who have found their can't not do and who operate from a committed, focused foundation. I've witnessed it over and over and over again. When you connect your internal passion to the right networks of people, you can go so much farther together.

Learning to Connect

Two of my favorite books are *The Tipping Point* by Malcolm Gladwell[7] and *Tribes* by Seth Godin.[8] Gladwell (www.gladwell .com) wrote, "Connectors are the people in a community who know large numbers of people and who are in the habit of making introductions. A connector is essentially the social equivalent of a computer network hub. They usually know people across an array of social, cultural, professional, and economic circles, and make a habit of introducing people who work or live in different circles. They are people who link us up with the world . . . people with a special gift for bringing the world together."

That's part of your job description in this social change work. Go do it as best you can. You may not already fit that description or ever become a full-blown Gladwell version, but it's a good goal. Remember, you don't have to be the master connector to learn lessons that you can apply to your life.

If I'm a fan of Gladwell's, I'm a superfan of Seth Godin (www .sethgodin.com/sg/). There are lots of people out there trying to tell stories well; he tells them very well. He also lives what he talks about; he's not just a good storyteller. Seth cares deeply about living in and contributing to a better world. He is his own version of a regular hero. I had the pleasure of having coffee with him in New York City last year and I've never written down that many notes that fast. Why I didn't audio record our conversation I'll never know.

The end result of being a great connector is, in short, a stronger, bigger, better tribe. Seth explains: "A tribe is a group of people connected to one another, connected to a leader, and connected to an idea. . . . A group needs only two things to be a tribe: a shared interest and a way to communicate." Everything in this book will, I hope, help you find your shared interest and the way to communicate.

He has two great notes that are totally relevant to being a connector, "What most people want in a leader is something that's very difficult to find: we want someone who *listens*. . . . President Reagan impressed his advisors, his adversaries, and his voters by *actively listening*. People want to be sure you hear what they said, they're less focused on whether or not you *do* what they said." That last sentence is worth reading again.

And, "If your work requires success before commitment, it will have neither. Part of leadership, a big part of it, actually, is the ability to stick with the dream for a long time. Long enough that the critics realize you're going to get there one way or another . . . so they follow." Active listening and determined optimism are core to being a great connector. Yes, stick with your dream for a long time, simply and beautifully put. Thanks, Malcolm and Seth, for spelling all this out so well.

Pacing the Floor Like an Expectant Father

David Griffis—we'll call him "Griff" like everyone else does—was born to be a connector. He has a degree in counseling and guidance. For over 35 years, in his consulting business, he worked with CEOs and their boards and teams, assisting with meeting facilitation, problem-solving, dispute resolution, and joint ventures. He and his wife, Ginnie, retired in Tucson where he has served on several nonprofit boards like the Tucson Pima Arts Council, Casa de los Ninos, and the Community Foundation for Southern Arizona. Griff and Ginnie were also early members of SVP Tucson, which has a focus on improving literacy and life skills for members of their community. He's another part-time can't-not-do person.

I can't say I know Griff really well, I've only met him twice; this story was pieced together from several people involved. But after hearing the story that follows I could see exactly how he was the right guy for the job at the right time. Even if, like me, you only met him twice, you would still feel the quiet, sunny confidence he exudes. No ego, not in it for himself, clearly. He's got a twinkle in his eyes, and listening to him recount his role and what he remembers is just fun. As with so many can't-not-do people, you can feel not only what he brought to the work, but what he gained from it; he lives and breathes the positives of being a great connector.

In 2011, five literacy-focused nonprofits in the Tucson area decided to explore a merger to create a single entity and they approached Griff to help figure out if it could be done. Before you start to think a merger between nonprofits might be easier than one between for-profits, think again. A few of the elements might look a little different, but it's still fundamentally about merging missions, people, cultures, programs, and products. It's tough stuff and, in the nonprofit sector, a merger usually happens only in response to either a leadership transition or a crisis in one organization.

So this case is unique because it was driven by aspiration, not transition or crisis. And even more unique because it was five, not two organizations. I'm not sure I've ever heard of that happening. And remember each organization has a director, maybe one or two key staff involved, and a board of probably about a dozen people. Griff wasn't just connecting five parts, he was connecting and holding together dozens of people. His task was to help them find their shared interests and provide the way to communicate (thanks again, Seth).

This whole process must have taken at least a year, maybe longer, right? Nope, seven months. Because there was a connector intertwined in and underneath all of it. A connector keeping detailed notes so all conversations were clear and could be referenced. A connector talking to individual people about their concerns and nudging them back into the fold. A connector listening and asking the right question when it needed to be asked, making sure important, tough issues didn't go unaddressed or end up being dealt with in the hallway, in a side conversation outside the real meeting.

Griff said, "My role was to keep the group together, focused on exploring common interests . . . facilitating the meetings and working behind the scenes to find language that would work for each entity . . . serving as a neutral convener . . . and pacing the floor like an expectant father until I heard the merger was approved by the fifth and final organization." That's the mindset, the essence of a connector.

There is a new entity in Tucson now. Literacy Connects (www .literacyconnects.org) represents $1 + 1 + 1 + 1 + 1 =$ much more than 5 and possesses so much more capacity and leverage to be a "more powerful voice to promote literacy in all its forms."

In its words, Literacy Connects is about how "we, as individuals, neighborhoods, organizations and businesses, share a human connection around literacy that helps each of us learn, grow, and have a voice. Together, we are developing more resources, serving more people, doing more good, and accomplishing more than ever before." That's the reason we all do this work, isn't? More people doing more good, that's what Griff's connecting made possible.

■ ■ ■

I truly believe in the power of human networks to solve our most intractable, seemingly unsolvable problems in the world. But these networks need the connectors, the open system people, the people who are wired to connect and keep connecting until the problem is solved or sustained momentum is in place.

You might be a connector/leader from the front of the pack, from the back of the parade, or walking alongside. You're not going as far as you could if you are not being a connector—as much of one as you can possibly be. I know not everyone is wired that way, so do your best. Always be motivated by, always be looking for ways to make $1 + 1 = 3$.

For you geeks, I remember a trigonometry lesson in school where we were taught that the interior angles of a triangle always add up to 180 degrees. That's true as long as that triangle is on a flat surface, but if you inscribe a triangle on a sphere, the angles add up to 270. Connecting people is about creating more possibilities by looking at the world in three-dimensional, not two-dimensional, form.

One last point—it is often the relationships with others that help each of us clarify our own internal values and identity. It's the outside that pulls out the inside and the inside that anchors and informs where we reach out. There is powerful stuff inside each of us when we connect it to the right people around us.

I've said it before; there are solutions out there, way more than people know, to most of our social challenges. I do not think our biggest challenge is know-how; it's not even money. It's connecting the right people with the right ideas in the right way. Sound easy? It must not be because the condition of our world today proves that it isn't.

Director or Connector?

I didn't change my job title from executive director to executive
connector just for the heck of it. Somewhere along this journey, I
realized two things: I don't do very much directing and the right
people who have or can find the answers are already out there, they
just need to be connected. That doesn't mean anything we are working
on is a quick fix. It just means we have most everything we need in
our heads and hearts and communities, right now, if we will work
relentlessly to connect these resources like Ms. Reece and her teachers
or Mr. Maple and the pins on his wall.

Connections have been a fundamental element of growing SVP
from the great idea of a few people in 1997 to a worldwide
movement. If someone asked me for a quick list of the top six tips
and tricks I've learned, and am constantly learning, about connecting,
I'd rattle off something like this:

1. It's about *dogged, stubborn persistence*. Nothing sexy, just keep at it.
   In my work to get people connected into SVP, so far the longest
   time it's taken to get someone to join our network is 11 years. I'm
   sure we'll break that record soon.
2. *Keep track* of every person (okay, maybe 98 percent) with whom
   you come in contact. You need to have a database, literally, where
   you keep track of them, the notes on your conversations, anything
   and everything. You never know which person you talked to
   X years ago will become the key missing link tomorrow.
3. *Keep in contact* with as many people as you can with some regularity.
   Even if, for many, it's just the occasional e-mail, text, or note to
   keep the connection going; it's worth it.
4. *Use social media* to reconnect with people whose contact information you've lost. More often than not, one of your friends knows
   where the person went or how to find them today. If you work

hard enough, there's almost no one you can't find via LinkedIn, Google, or Facebook.

5. *Connect at the heart*, not just the head, level. There are facts and figures that connect us, but more than anything, stories and hearts connect us for the long haul.

6. Whenever you meet someone or are in a meeting or room with other people, *stop and think who else* should this person, these people, be connected to? Just make it a habit.

Five Key Ideas from Chapter 6

1. It is only by asking questions and actively listening that you can become a great connector. You will discover more and more interplay between these seven questions.

2. Connecting creates more potential, more possibilities, more relationships.

3. You can be a great connector from the front of the pack, from the back of the parade, or walking alongside. You can also do so by being a servant leader or occasionally using your own bully pulpit, when needed.

4. You may not be wired to be a great connector, but do your best. That's true of all seven questions, no one can be great at *all* of them, but everyone can be great for *some* of them.

5. You don't have to do it all yourself, in fact, you can't. So do your part, the part you do best, and connect to lots of other people who do those other parts better than you do.

PART III

Bringing It All Together for Your World and You

CHAPTER 7

Heidi Breeze-Harris, a Sick Pregnant Lady with an Idea

What Is Your Can't Not Do?

All men dream, but not equally. Those who dream by night in the dusty recesses of their minds wake up in the day to find it was vanity, but the dreamers of the day are dangerous people, for they may act on their dreams with open eyes, to make it possible.

—T.S. Eliot

Fistula leaves a hole in a mother's bladder or rectum, which causes leakage of urine or feces. It affects more than 2 million women and girls in the developing world. Fistulas develop when a woman's childbirth is obstructed during labor and she doesn't have access to medical care. These mothers are not only irreparably physically damaged for life but are frequently pushed to the edges of African society, socially ostracized, unable to board a bus, share a meal, or even pray communally. It's so sickening in so many ways.

I met Heidi Breeze-Harris about 12 years ago. It was another rainy Seattle night. We were both at a lecture to hear Kathy Calvin of the United Nations Foundation. Kathy was in town to talk about the foundation's work to eradicate fistula. When I sat down with Heidi for coffee earlier this year to talk about her work, she told me, "When I first heard about fistula, I thought it was something that should be gone; it's a terrible injustice that *must* go away." On that evening 12 years ago, Heidi, who was one month pregnant, said to Kathy afterward, "I'm just a sick pregnant lady with an idea . . ." and they exchanged business cards.

In some ways, Heidi's story is the most improbable of all, but it's about a person, a regular hero, who lived as normal and unfamous a life as anyone. She had several successful professional chapters in her life, but she didn't have a bunch of money or extra time on her hands. Yet, many people would think that fulfilling her can't not do would have only been possible if she had millions of dollars and all the time in the world to pull it off. Just the opposite was true.

A month after that evening with Kathy Calvin, Heidi was largely confined to bed, sick from the early stages of her first pregnancy. She did a lot of reading and TV watching. While she was lying in bed, she was struck by one of those fluky coincidences. Three different sources were all talking about fistula, the same issue she had decided to work on when she serendipitously met Kathy Calvin. "Yeah, I was lying in bed and I had heard about it three times in a week. I'm somebody who believes if you hear something and it enters your consciousness more than two or three times in a reasonable span of time, you should pay attention."

The first source of information was *Ms. Magazine*, which named Catherine Hamelin, founder of the Addis Ababa Fistula Hospital (http://hamlinfistula.org/), as their woman of the year. Dr. Hamelin just turned 90, by the way, and she is still on the job. Then, *The*

Washington Post published an article about fistula. And, finally, Oprah had a show that covered the issue, and highlighted Dr. Hamelin's work. Thousands of viewers were compelled to act and Dr. Hamelin's foundation received more than $3 million in donations. Some people donate money; that's a very good thing. Some people were compelled to act. Heidi was compelled to try to solve the problem.

Back when Heidi met Kathy that rainy evening in Seattle, she asked if the UN Foundation might be willing to partner with her on an idea she was hatching, aimed at getting more people involved in the fight against fistula. Heidi explained, "I worked with one person at the UN Foundation and one person from the United Nations Fund for Population Activities [UNFPA], which had launched their program two years before. I felt like the campaign at UNFPA was the place I could best use my social capital. They weren't just doing treatments, they were implementing prevention programs and weren't just in one country. They were the only ones that felt like they were addressing the whole picture so I basically laid in bed having conference calls twice a week with these people, because that was all I could do during eight months of bed rest."

On August 26, 2004, her bed rest abruptly ended and Heidi delivered her baby, Coleman. After 18 hours of labor, a three-hour delay in locating a bed at a hospital during a major nursing strike in Seattle, and a nightmare drive across the 520 bridge during rush hour to a hospital in Kirkland, Coleman entered the world via emergency C-section. Eight hours later, Heidi was wheeled back into emergency surgery due to a massive hemorrhage. A fairly simple 30-minute cauterization turned into a five hour ordeal with substantial blood loss and 7 pints of blood transfused into her to keep her alive. She was 40 minutes from full kidney failure.

The cause? A long labor due to cephalopelvic disproportion; her baby was bigger than her pelvic opening. She had an obstructed delivery. Heidi suffered the *very same* ordeal as the women she was hoping to help in Africa. If she had been in a developing country, she likely would have died. At a minimum, the rest of her life would have been drastically altered for the worse. Her work was now, for some less than desirable reasons, very connected to who she was at her core.

Can you even begin to fathom the doubts and fears she must have felt after the trauma of Coleman's birth? Most people would take some time to heal and appreciate life. But not Heidi. She went back and forth to Kenya, halfway around the world, to create One By One (now www.fightfistula.org) to build public health programs, create awareness, and inspire a movement to eradicate fistula. It reminds me of Jeff Carr and his unusual move to make inner city kids in Los Angeles part of the solution at the most dangerous parks in the middle of the night.

Heidi says, "I was enthusiastic about helping to end fistula before this happened to me, but afterward the cause was even more real for me because I had my own experience of the pain of this kind of labor. And the suffering, isolation, and loss these women experience in the aftermath is overwhelming for me to imagine. I felt like I had to use my energy. I remember I was calling the UN Foundation three weeks after Coleman was born, and they were wondering why I was on the phone with them so soon after my experience. And there I was feeling so bad that it had been three whole weeks since I had done something and I was so sorry."

"I just couldn't . . . couldn't not do it (her words, verbatim). I just felt this . . . I can't even describe it, this kooky sort of drive. Even with a new infant I was like, I have to do this thing." If that isn't what determined optimism sounds like, I don't know what does. Couldn't not do it.

When you talk with Heidi, there is a sort of incongruity you feel—this very normal, regular next-door neighbor juxtaposed with what she took on and how far she had to go to do it. And yet, that is one of the key points I hope you take away from this book: uncommon good comes from exceptionally common people; in fact, those are the people who are going to make the biggest difference. There are a whole lot more Heidis and Griffs than there are philanthropically minded billionaires and movie stars. Given the power of social multipliers, the impact each of us can now have, like Heidi did, is largely up to each of us.

Needless to say, someone like Heidi is a pretty extreme, in the positive sense, role model. Do we all have to suffer a near-death experience and travel halfway around the world when we find our can't not do? No. Don't get stuck thinking you have to go as far as Heidi or let her story make this all feel unattainable. The lessons are about how she felt about the work and why and how she did it. She is an ordinary person who has given her life to an extraordinary cause.

Over 10 years Heidi raised more than $3.5 million for fistula treatment, prevention, reintegration, and education. Those funds educated over 300,000 rural people, screened over 4,500 women for fistula, and have helped to heal more than 2,000 women. Based on their pilot project in Kenya called "Let's End Fistula," Heidi's work changed the way a comprehensive fistula program is designed and the program is now being scaled up. One By One contributed greatly to the overall awareness and resources for fistula and maternal health programs through its work with the U.S. Congress and UNFPA.

Looking to the future, One By One investments in Tanzania, Niger, and Ethiopia have trained hundreds of rural birth attendants and community health workers who are helping women get the prenatal care and medical attention they need to survive childbirth and have a healthy baby. Most of the women with fistula helped by One By One would not have been helped in any other way.

And one more thing Heidi told me: "As a result of the amazing people with whom I have had the honor to work alongside, my leadership capacity has grown and changed dramatically." Change the world . . . and change yourself.

A footnote to Heidi's story: just a few months ago, I was copied on an e-mail she sent around explaining that she needed to take a break and step back from the work for a while after more than 10 very impactful years. When I talk about committing, for the long-term, to one can't not do in your life, 10-plus years, especially at Heidi's pace, definitely meets the mark. Dwight Frindt is in his 38th year of focusing on ending hunger; we don't all have to commit 38 years, and most of us won't. There's no single standard to apply to "long-term," but if each of us can commit deeply for 10 years at a time to one cause, it will add up to a profound effect on the world.

What's the Point?

These people don't just have a can-do attitude, they have a can't-not-do mindset. They've found that work, that cause in their life that they can't not do. Yes, the grammar is off. My eighth-grade English teacher, Mrs. McLaren, would be screeching at me for saying it that way. The double negative connotes they are doubly, or more, committed. The seven questions culminate in this one.

You either find this can't-not-do feeling or you do not, and it might not be now or yet, but I deeply hope it will be someday for each of you. It is what gets you off the sidelines and into the action. This feeling is what sustains you when all looks impossible. It pushes you into the hard places. The problems each of these regular heroes is addressing are hard, yet they throw themselves—their hearts, brains, and resources—at the problems.

People told me that to not do what they are doing would be criminal, cowardly, and that they'd be a charade. The problem at hand is, Heidi told me, "something that must be gone." There is a sense of being compelled to do the good work they are endeavoring to do. It's about a core sense of self. It becomes part of who you are, your identity, someday part of your legacy. It gives people a more expansive, forwarded-thinking self-image. When you find your can't not do it changes who you are, for yourself and for the world.

The first time my friend, Larry, heard me talk about this, he blogged something like, "So do those double negatives simply resolve themselves into 'what can you do'? No, much, much more. Those words are asking us to find that thing in our life that is so powerful, irresistible, and unavoidable that we feel we have no choice but to pursue it. They ask us to look beyond the potential of 'I can,' beyond the moral force of 'I should,' even further on past the imperative of 'I must do.' All those words—can, should, must—leave things in our hands. We can deny them, but what pursuit, what cause could we not deny under any conditions?"

Please remember this, I've said it before, some can't-not-do people, like Lisa Chin, have shifted their whole careers. Some have committed serious time, but not full time, like Kevin Shaw. Some have carved out some extra hours in a week alongside a career, like Kerry McClenahan. This type of change does demand focused time, but the amount of time depends on where you are in your life. You may not have lots of time right now, but someday you'll have more. Or maybe you are ready to make the time right now, after you think about these seven questions. What matters most is the intensity and longevity of your focus on the challenge.

A Different Kind of Career Dedicated to Can't Not Do

This may seem a little off-track, but stick with me. My hobby is refereeing high school basketball. It's not my job, it's not my cause in life, but I am passionate about it. The feeling of being in a packed high school gym on a Friday night, the band playing, the coaches and fans yelling, it just gets the adrenaline pumping and requires a focus that's pretty unique for about an hour and a half. And there is a camaraderie with your two fellow refs; it's the three of us against the world for a little while.

I have a handful of friends whose dream is to referee in the NBA. I've done a summer camp with a couple current NBA refs, know another guy who looks like he's on his way, and a couple more who have committed themselves to doing so. They have a sort of kooky drive to make it to the big time. I don't think any of them would have imagined this when they were growing up, though there was probably a love of the game of basketball that is part of their core. I know it's part of mine; I love the game. At some point, it became their passion, their cause, if you will, in life.

Maybe they are not changing the world, but they can't not do it. These individuals have day jobs, but they can't wait to get back to the time they commit to becoming great referees and, believe me, it takes a lot of hours. They can't get it out of their heads. There are people who find what they can't not do in all walks of life in all kinds of endeavors; we're just focused in this book on the ones who want to change the world. But I share the story to perhaps give some readers another way to connect and relate to and understand the core feeling, the impulse that underlies can't not do.

Can't Not Do for Others

William was born 10 weeks premature with a diagnosis of hydro-cephalus or water on the brain. It's a condition in which fluid accumulates in the cavities of the brain. If the pressure isn't relieved, it can cause intracranial pressure, progressive enlargement of the head, and mental disability. It can also cause death.

Sometimes the road to a can't-not-do passion is obvious, as in Heidi's experience, and sometimes something so awful happens to us that we can't stand the thought of it happening to someone else. I have met some phenomenal people through my work with Social Venture Partners. They all have a story. Some are about "wanting to do more because . . ." or "I think this is where I want to have an impact." And then you meet someone like Paul Gross, with a beautiful infant son like William.

Paul can be a very intense guy and yet, underneath that part of his personality, you can also feel a genuine, emotional human being.

He conveys a very purposeful energy in everything he does, but I can feel a warm-hearted part of him right alongside the intensity. I suspect he's always working to find a balance between those parts of who he is.

William's first few days were filled with one medical crisis after another. He spent his first month in the intensive care unit and didn't go home until he was two months old. I've had three boys, two of their births were by C-section. One of the births did get a little dicey for a few minutes, but in the end, nothing even remotely approaching what Paul and his wife, Lori, had to go through for months, for a lifetime really.

There is no cure for hydrocephalus; the treatment is surgery to implant a shunt in the brain to ease the pressure. It's very scary when your newborn undergoes surgery and just as scary afterward; Paul and Lori watched William have a grand mal seizure after one surgery. It's one of those nightmares that every parent prays will never happen to their little ones. They knew that William could be facing frequent emergency brain surgery.

The specifics of William's diagnosis aren't as much the focus here as is Paul and Lori's reaction to it. When the two of them researched the treatments, outcomes, and the current state of research, like parents do when faced with a medical crisis, they were despondent with what they learned. Paul learned that the shunt has the highest failure rate of any medically implanted device; 50 percent fail within the first two years. Paul explained, "The shunt was created in 1952 by the father of a child with hydrocephalus. While it saved lives, it seemed to stall the drive to research better therapeutic interventions or find a cure. The shunt manufacturers had made only minor incremental improvements to this failure-prone device. Outcomes were dismal with below average IQs and 60 percent of the children not being able to live independently in adulthood."

In short, there was not enough research going on, and much of what was being done was not connected, a common problem in the often-siloed scientific world. There were simple protocols that could be implemented that would make a difference in the delivery room, and there were several organizations working on the issue, but mostly in isolation. It struck Paul that he might have the opportunity to prevent this same outcome for countless other newborns in the future, for families he would never know and that would never know William. If you had that opportunity . . . how could you not?

If you knew Paul, you'd know he is the kind of person who, if he makes up his mind, makes things happen. He looked at the fragmented, disconnected efforts to develop a better shunt and decided the best approach would be to "get all the wood behind one arrow." It meant moving a unique collection of researchers, doctors, and government agencies, and it would take a whole new set of skills and behaviors that he wasn't used to using.

Paul had to put a whole new value on group dynamics, not as in how do you convince a group of your idea, something at which he was very good, but rather, how to help everyone in the system work better collectively, something he wasn't as good at . . . yet. He knew he could only get from Point A to Point B if everyone came along as a group. He had to be a connector. As he related to me, "I think impatience is a delicate edge. Without it you have complacence. With too much of it, you have overdrive in a bad way. I think finding the right balance has taken a childish impetuousness and turned it into a positive force."

He also admits he had to get over a fear of failing. This was a big goal, a big project with a lot of very powerful, entrenched people and systems and it was intimidating, to say the least. How many of us would not fear failing in that scenario? I don't see many hands go up, nor is mine.

But overcoming that fear was what it took to start moving a whole system to do a better job of taking care of newborns that might have hydrocephalus. This is what I mean when I say this feeling of can't not do is what sustains you when all looks impossible. The problems are really, really hard. For Paul, it was worth overcoming his fears and insecurities for the next newborn he could help.

Today, Paul spends parts of his week being an advocate and board leader for changes in the system that will change new lives. At hospitals that are piloting the new program, the infection rate, the most devastating complication of a shunt, has been reduced by 35 percent for newborns treated with the new protocol. Imagine how many lives will be changed and made profoundly better.

And a footnote about Paul, along the lines of Eleuthera and Heidi, he has taken everything he's learned about hydrocephalus and now he's applying his energy part-time to the fight against cerebral palsy (CP). He's about to join a key board of the largest private funder of CP research and is organizing a National Institutes of Health workshop that will pull together experts to shape treatments collectively. He told me he is "making much more progress than with hydrocephalus because of what he has learned and done [with hydrocephalus]." If you don't just stop right here and say "wow, that's really cool," check your pulse. That's what hard-core, can't-not-do people do. Paul put 10 years into hydrocephalus, and he's not done. But now he is going to focus his time and commitment to go deep in another area and leverage what he's learned. That's upper-level can't-not-do-ness.

Can't Not Do Takes Time, a Long Time

Finding what you can't not do is about finding what you can be passionate about and commit to for the long term, for several years, maybe even the rest of your life. There are lots of causes in your community and your world that you could get involved in because someone else asked you to or that might take an afternoon here or there. Nothing wrong with that per se, but it's not what is going to change your community and your world for the better. We have enough human and financial capital; we just let it get too splintered over the years.

If it helps to have one more example of what happens with long-term, singular focus, consider this. In 1978 a handful of Rotarians (www.rotary.org) decided polio was a problem they didn't just *want* to help solve, but they came to believe they *had to* solve. They were regular heroes, they just didn't know it at the time. By 1999, polio was still endemic in about 20 countries, over 10,000 cases worldwide. But a handful of people had already decided, 21 years before, that eradicating polio wasn't something they could do; it was something they couldn't not do. Today, polio is endemic in a handful countries and the end game, though still very difficult, is within sight. Because of the Gates Foundation, the Centers for Disease Control, UNICEF, the WHO, and of course, Rotary, ending polio is not just something we can do, now it's something we can't not do.

Consider the world today if that handful of Rotarians had let "seemingly impossible" or "really hard" stop them 38 years ago or anywhere along this journey. Why does 38 years ring so familiar to me? Millions of lives around the world are different today because those individuals decided what they would commit to for the long term, for the rest of some of their lives. I can't overstate how important this is. If you look underneath the most vexing problems in the world that eventually get solved, you'll almost always find a few people, later joined by more people somewhere along the way, who committed for the long term to what they can't not do. If more, if enough people take this pathway in the future who knows what we can accomplish?

What Is It in Your Life That You Can't Not Do?

There's a reason I phrase this question in a quirky and grammatically challenged way. It's because those are the words many, many people used, verbatim. There must have been a reason why they put it that way. I think it's because the question, phrased that way, makes you twist your mind and your heart a little. It gets your attention. It's harder to let go of can't not do than can do. It forces you to dig deeper for your answer, to find your conviction.

What is your can't not do is *the* fundamental question. I believe this so deeply because I've watched and learned it from thousands of people, around the world, for 17 years. This isn't a theory or a research project, it comes from deeply personal, on-the-ground experiences. It's messy human work, full of small successes and just as many failures.

To reiterate, the people who dare to open their hearts and ask themselves this question and authentically answer it are the ones who will truly create change. I know that it takes more than just a question to make change happen, but the right question challenges us to take the first step and then bigger steps. It guides us down a pathway to having more impact on the world . . . and on our own lives.

Finding and owning your can't not do is an assertion of faith in your capacity to help create a better world. It is an expression of the power of an intentional life. It's an unambiguous, unapologetic expression of optimism. What each of us does, how we live our lives matters, not a little bit but a lot. It truly matters. I hope you will be ready to realize more of your potential, to dig more deeply into that question, to find your can't not do in this life.

Five Key Ideas from Chapter 7

1. Don't get stuck thinking that you need to be someone who goes to the ends of the earth like Heidi or is famous like Martin Luther King, Jr. or Mother Theresa to help create real change in this world. The point is to *learn* from each of them. What lessons can you take away from each of their lives that you can adapt and apply to your life?

2. Some of the people in this book shifted their whole careers, some found a few hours a week for an extended period, and others devoted time that fell somewhere in between.

3. What matters most is the intensity, singularity, and longevity of your focus or use of your professional talents applied to the social challenge or cause that fits you best.

4. You can't dictate change to a community or a group; you have to be a connector and bring as many people as possible to the table.

5. What is it in your life that you can't not do? This is the fundamental question.

CHAPTER 8

Why *Your* Social Drives Matter More Now

The Equation

Nothing in the world can take the place of persistence. Talent will not; nothing is more common than unsuccessful men with talent. Genius will not; unrewarded genius is almost a proverb. Education will not; the world is full of educated derelicts. Persistence and determination alone are omnipotent. The slogan Press On! has solved and always will solve the problems of the human race.

—Calvin Coolidge

Union City and Newark, New Jersey, are less than 10 miles apart, along I-95 just across the Hackensack River from each other. High unemployment and chronic poverty exist in both cities. Back in the 1980s, in fact, Union City's school district was at risk of a New Jersey state takeover, given how poorly its schools were performing. Union City is one of those cities with a great manufacturing history; it was once known as the Embroidery Capital of the United States.

Over the past five years, Newark got an incremental infusion of well over $100 million of external philanthropic funds into its public schools, And yet Union City is the school district that has made more gains in student achievement. More than 90 percent of the city's students receive free or reduced lunch and three-fourths speak a language other than English at home. It makes no sense. Why would the two districts perform much differently in the first place, given how similar the conditions are? And if either district were to improve, shouldn't it be the one receiving all the extra funding from outside the system?

Today, Union City has high school graduation rates near 90 percent, more than 10 points higher than the national average; 60 percent of students go on to college; and achievement scores throughout the school system far exceed what would be expected given the city's demographics and socioeconomic situation. Some of this is detailed in Professor David Kirp's book, *Improbable Scholars*.[1]

Union City hasn't implemented a massive, expensive school reform plan. Rather there was a series of seemingly mundane things that made the difference, things like full-day preschool for all children, word-soaked classrooms with a rich feel for language, immigrant kids becoming fluent first in their native language and then in English, analyses of students' test scores to diagnose and address problems, and several more blocking and tackling elements.

Connections, that is, making $1 + 1 = 3$, is one of the key elements running through everything. The school system built a structure that connects effective teachers, parents, students and curriculum; there is collaboration among teachers, and an emphasis on connecting parents as vital partners in their children's education. Principals like Mr. Bennetti at Union City High School and teachers like Ms. Alina Bossbaly, third grade, make all the difference. Bossbaly is such a good teacher they've coined a term for her kind of teaching: "Bossbaly-izing" children. She is also a mentor and coach to many of her peers, one of the key success factors. They are changing lives every day, just like Anne Reece and her teachers are at White Center Elementary. As Prof. Kirp concluded, "nationwide, there's no reason school districts—big or small, predominantly white, Latino, black—cannot construct a system that, like the schools of Union City, bends the arc of children's lives."

■ ■ ■

Nationally, the level of educational attainment at public schools in the United States in the past two generations has ground to a halt, no matter how many solutions we try or how much money we spend. And yet, there are Union Citys and White Centers to be found throughout the United States, proving that we do have solutions to seemingly intractable challenges. We clearly have a long way to go in seeing public education overall change its flat trajectory of student performance, but the biggest challenge is *not* a lack of solutions to the problems at hand. *We have solutions.*

And not only do they exist, but the biggest barrier is rarely a lack of funding. Over the past 40 years, the rate of spending per student in U.S. public schools has doubled, in real dollars, with no appreciable improvement in student achievement. All over the country, school districts and governments have rarely hesitated to increase the investment in schools, a noble instinct to be sure, but one with limited effect on children's academic performance and lives. *We have funding.*

The Equation

Union City is simply one more reiteration of two simple, vital facts: (1) we have solutions to many social challenges, far more than most people think, and (2) we have a significant amount of financial resources to invest in ameliorating those challenges (and more, new sources of capital are coming into play, via impact investing). Combine those two facts with the new dynamics we discussed in the Introduction about social multipliers and we now have just about everything we need to make significant social progress in the next generation.

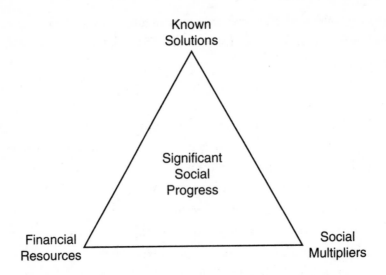

What makes that equation add up for our communities and ecosystems? The answer is almost inescapable, and it's what this whole book has been about. The variables in that equation are like tools that people can put to highest and best use in their communities. This book is full of stories of can't-not-do people who became the leaders or one of the missing pieces that helped put this equation to work and contributes to positive social progress.

People like Jeff Carr and Eleuthera Lisch, who tackled inner city violence; and Anne Reece and Ms. Bossbaly, who pursued academic achievement; David Risher and his fight against third-world illiteracy; Lisa Chin and Jeff Tollefson, who worked to create better opportunities and lives for youth. I could go on and on. Make no mistake, every one of these people would be the first to tell you they are only one of hundreds, thousands, that make real change possible (that's why they are great listeners and connectors), but their individual impact is just as certain.

That sounds almost too simplistic in this complex world, doesn't it? Not really, because there was nothing simple in how these people you've read about made an outsized difference; it's hard work, they had to go to hard places. Sometimes it takes many years to truly distill what you are a determined optimist about and to become an active listener. Time and time and time again, what makes the difference are can't-not-do people who focus for the long term on that one cause; we just need more and more of them. That belief is the reason why Bill and Melinda Gates created www.globalcitizen.org.

What's unique today is the existence of that Solutions + Resources + Multipliers equation. The solutions and resources have been accelerating over the past 25 to 50 years and the multipliers have largely been added to the equation in the past 10 years. In short, that's why your social drive, why finding your can't not do matters more now than it ever has.

What's Possible

One of my favorite TED talks of all time is Peter Diamandis, "Abundance Is Our Future."[2] In part, he talks about the future, but he begins by taking a quick tour through progress made in the past hundred years—the average human lifespan has more than doubled, childhood mortality has come down by a factor of 10, and global literacy has gone from 25 percent to over 80 percent, and people like David Risher are working on that last 10 to 20 percent.

We've talked about teen pregnancy and violent crime declining by half in the past 40 years, and gang violence down significantly in some, though not all, cities across the United States. If you need more evidence, visit Blueprints for Healthy Youth Development (www.blueprintsprograms.com) and click on Blueprints Programs; you will find dozens of the most rigorously evaluated programs with positive effects on young peoples' behavior. All of that progress still leaves major social challenges where we have *not* made the same kind of progress. But if we could focus our resources and time, more can't-not-do people will put that social progress equation to work, and together we could, over the next generation:

- Bend the arc of education toward the positive. We've been stuck for nearly 50 years, but we have the solutions to implement early childhood education across all of our communities, improve reading, math, and science achievement by our students, and increase our graduation rates significantly.

- Change the foster care system so fewer kids go in, more kids get the right outcomes when they are in the system, and more young people exit the system sooner and with more positive outcomes. And we'd save untold societal costs downstream as well.
- Make homelessness increasingly rare and on its way to being a relic of the past.
- Finally start to see rates of poverty in the United States decline below 15 percent and move toward single-digit percentages. No matter what your politics, ameliorating poverty is an example of a social challenge in which we've invested trillions of public dollars, with no apparent effect.
- I could go on and on . . .

If any of the statements above feel implausible or unlikely to you, then think back to what people must have felt about teen pregnancy and violent crime 40 years ago, or about gang violence just 10 years ago. Just to drive the point all the way home, two more significant examples come to mind of what is possible, in spite of the odds and expectations.

Massachusetts was the first state to approve marriage equality in 2004. At that time, further progress looked like a mountain beyond Everest, the backlash was extraordinary. In reaction, a group of funders and activists launched a shared game plan, with long-term funding and collaborative messaging. Ten years later in 2015, it seems almost unimaginable that over 35 states, and counting, have now enacted marriage equality laws. It's just about passed a tipping point, much like the eradication of polio.

And for three decades, conservative political strategists have mounted an extraordinary effort to reshape public policy. The National Center for Responsive Philanthropy (www.ncrp.org) wrote a report that "documents the substantial role that 12 foundations played in developing and sustaining key institutions in the movement,"[3] looking back at 30 years of sustained, unrestricted funding. It has profoundly changed American politics.

In both of those cases, from different sides of the philosophical aisle, there were a handful of people and organizations that were undoubtedly determined optimists, knew who they were at their core, were ready and willing to stick with it through the hard places. They invested in known *solutions*, concentrated their *resources*, and leveraged those *multipliers* to great *social progress*.

Today's challenges, while tough, are happening when we are wealthier, more connected, more innovative, and more amplified than at any time in human history. And we live in a world with the inspiring quantity and quality of solutions, resources, and multipliers that exist today. Each of us can now put those to use in fundamentally new and world-changing ways. It is an incredible time to find your can't not do.

■ ■ ■

The pathway to more and more people finding their can't not do is not a mystery or black hole. This book lays it out for you in a tangible, accessible way. The pathway is there for you to travel, if and when you are ready, willing, and able. The potential to tip the balance toward significant positive—or negative—change has never been greater. You can be a lever tipping that balance.

So what's your can't not do? I've already said, this is *the* fundamental question. It's right there for you to seize. It's not easy, but to help change the world does not require superhuman abilities or special destinies, it requires the combination of a personal drive to make a difference with deliberate reflection on some key questions, seven of them, and turning your answers into action. Drive, reflection, action. If that sounds simple, it's not. If it sounds attainable, it is.

And if it sounds universal, it truly is. When I was in China last year, I asked Jiawen Shu at SVP China if can't not do translates and she said, in Chinese it reads as "some motivation in your core to make you devote to or feel responsible for something. It's a phrase expressing stronger passion than must-do." Stronger passion than must-do. I love that. If each of us will find that one cause that we can't not do, we will each be a powerful lever that tips the balance toward a better and better world.

Five Key Ideas from Chapter 8

1. For almost every social challenge, knowing the right solution is rarely the biggest barrier.
2. Known Solutions + Financial Resources + Social Multipliers = Significant Social Progress!
3. There is enough wealth and resources, but they are either untapped or used inefficiently. Can't-not-do connectors are the critical missing ingredient; we need more.
4. Now is the best time in human history to tackle these challenges; it's never been better.
5. In Chinese, can't not do translates to "a stronger passion than must do."

CONCLUSION

Surrendering to the Intention

This is the true joy in life, the being used for a purpose recognized by yourself as a mighty one; the being thoroughly worn out before you are thrown on the scrap heap; the being a force of nature instead of a feverish selfish little clod of ailments and grievances complaining that the world will not devote itself to making you happy.

—George Bernard Shaw

Every once in a while you sit down to talk to someone and you just feel like you have a mind-meld, that person is so in tune with what you're thinking and you can't write down his ideas fast enough. It was that way when I had coffee with Dwight Frindt. I ran back out to my car to get my notepad because what I thought would be a five-minute conversation turned into over an hour. For Dwight, whom you first met in Chapter One, his work with The Hunger Project is "about surrendering to the intention that is wanting to use his life." What a powerful notion, that a cause for social change is wanting to use his life, each of our lives. I love that. If each of us, all of us, will find that one cause that we will surrender ourselves to it will make a world of difference and we will have a different world.

One of the most important reasons to talk about the seven questions by looking at about 20 different stories is because everyone, and I mean every one, can see yourself in at least one or two, probably more, of these stories. Maybe you don't relate to all of them or even many of them, but I know you can relate to at least one can't-not-do story (check Appendix 3, too).

Dwight certainly didn't have to quit his day job, but he did decide to change his life. And in so doing, it changed him profoundly. This is really important to know. In order to *get* more out of life, you have to *give* more to life. Go find your can't not do, like Dwight did. And when you do, you will not only give more, you will get more, way more back, and your own life will be changed.

A Meaningful versus a Happy Life

There is a tension between a meaningful and a happy life that we've touched on already. They're not mutually exclusive, but if you are going to tilt one way, tilt toward meaningful because, done with sustained commitment, a meaningful life can eventually lead to a happy life. I'm not sure about the other way around. This is not a self-help book, it's a help-the-world book. But let me bring it full circle and make the strong case that the best, most powerful way to help yourself is to help the world. Here are three different, short anecdotes that reinforce that virtuous cycle and the value of a meaningful life lived, in part, through your can't not do.

First, from the world of *research*, let's revisit a few more key things learned from the research mentioned earlier and reported in the *Journal of Positive Psychology* on key differences between a *happy life* and a *meaningful life*.[1] Just to reiterate, I'm not antihappy, but let me share a few more vital things they learned:

• Happiness is considerably more short-lived and fleeting than meaningfulness.

- Happiness is largely present-oriented, where meaningfulness involves integrating past, present, and future. Present events in life draw value from future possibilities, which we will need when facing a big challenge ahead, like defining and living your can't not do.
- Having sufficient money to purchase objects of desire is important for happiness but makes essentially no difference as to whether a life is meaningful.
- Challenges may reduce present happiness but are linked to much higher future meaningfulness.
- Happiness is linked to being a taker rather than a giver, meaningfulness is the opposite.

Next, from the *spiritual* world, a perspective on happy versus meaningful from Eknath Easwaran (www.easwaran.org), a spiritual teacher, an author of books on meditation and ways to lead a fulfilling life, and a translator and interpreter of Indian literature. Easwaran says, "To think that we can pursue joy as a collector pursues butterflies, seeking it here and there, is folly. We can never go after joy because joy has got to come after us. It's like the horizon. When you look from the Berkeley hills, the horizon looks as if it is just beyond the Golden Gate. You honestly believe that if you go there, you will reach the horizon. . . .

"But as you pursue it, it recedes farther and farther, and that is the nature of pleasure. It peeps out from the store, the restaurant, the bank, but when you enter there you will find it recedes farther and farther. When we begin to seek a higher goal, for the welfare of our family and community (i.e. deeper meaning), joy slowly tiptoes after us. We don't have to say to joy, 'Excuse me, will you please come to my house?' Joy will come and put her suitcase down and say, 'I am going to be here, whether you like it or not.' That is how happiness comes."

And from the world of *health*, one more reason to believe that a meaningful life trumps a happy one—you'll be healthier. Barbara

Fredrickson, a psychological researcher at the University of North Carolina/Chapel Hill who specializes in positive emotions, and Steve Cole, a genetics and psychiatric researcher at UCLA, examined the self-reported levels of happiness and meaning in 80 research subjects.[2] Happiness was defined as feeling good. Meaning was defined as an orientation to something bigger than the self.

Cole and Fredrickson found that people who are happy but have little to no sense of meaning in their lives have the same gene expression patterns as people who are responding to and enduring chronic adversity. There is, in short, a more beneficial gene expression pattern associated with meaningfulness. It seems that feeling happy is not enough. People need meaning to thrive. In the words of Carl Jung, "The least of things with a meaning is worth more in life than the greatest of things without it." Jung's wisdom certainly seems to apply to our bodies, as well as to our hearts and our minds.

This work to help change the world isn't a one-way street, you won't end up just helping the world around you. When you really dig in, I promise you it is a two-way, purpose-infusing pathway through life. If you ask Heidi, Lisa, David, Eric, Eleuthera, or anyone in this book, I will bet my last dollar that each of them would give the same answers to three simple questions:

1. The greatest key to getting the most out of life? *Give yourself away in life.*
2. The best route to a happy life? *Live a life of meaning and purpose.*
3. The most sure-fire way to change your life? *Help change the world.*

It's a beautiful, virtuous, simple cycle, and it's available to each of us, at no cost other than time, blood, sweat, and tears—and digging into these seven questions. If you don't believe it yet, just try it; if I'm wrong, email me at shoe@paulshoemaker.org and tell me. I promise I'll call you up and talk about it.

If, by chance, you ask yourself the question, "What is my can't not do?" and decide, "Well, if I truly had a can't not do, I would have done it already, so I guess I don't have one," then let me suggest one more thing—try asking yourself, "If I learned I was going to die tomorrow, what would be my biggest regret regarding something I did not start and finish?" A friend of mine, Ben Klasky, put it this way, "If someone told me, 'I'm going to take your life and then the world will have peace forever,' just about any one of us would say, 'take me now.'" No, I'm not asking you to think about *that* question, but work back from that and ask, what might you regret, 10 years from now, that you didn't answer today? (If you have doubts and fears that hold you back, go to www.paulshoemaker.org for some helpful ideas about fears, uncertainties, and doubts.)

Let me share one last gem from my friend, Larry, who wrote this to me right before I finished the final review. He wrote, "to have a purpose is to be a part of something bigger, to have a reference point outside ourselves. So when we are called to something that is *meaningful*, it inherently creates a vantage outside our personal self-centered perspective. The question 'What is your can't not do?' puts you outside yourself as a spectator. The challenge is to figure out how to help a person feel like they are society's needs calling upon themselves. To be the caller and the called." To surrender to the intention.

Are you truly living a life full of potential and purpose or are you living a guarded life? Are you honoring a call to do something or suppressing something with rationalizations? Do you surround yourself with people who are wind in your sails or with people who talk you down from your dreams? The only reason I dare to ask questions like these is because my own answer to each question has been uncertain far too many times in life. I pose them not as a preacher but as someone living and breathing this journey with you, still struggling to find that life of deeper and deeper purpose and meaning.

Start the Journey

If you'd like some ideas on how to get started, let me offer you a few:

- Sit down with a good friend or a loved one, someone your trust, and throw out one or two of these questions over a beer or dinner and spend time sort of "marinating" in it. Talk it over. See what it makes you feel, how each of you might answer the question.
- Get together with a group—at home, at work, with your neighbors—and listen to and learn from how each person answers the questions. You will inevitably hear something you hadn't thought about and your potential will grow.
- If you're a writer, jot down your thoughts. Do some journaling, reflecting on a question or two at a time. Really take time to explore.
- Heck, write to me. I'll help or help connect you to other people wrestling with the same question(s).
- The questions are in a sequence, but any one of them can stand on its own, can be a runway for finding your can't not do. So pick a starting place, any place, maybe try to stay within the three parts of the book if you are jumping around. Maybe take one per week or one per month.
- No matter where or how you start, commit to turning your answers into action someday. Like Goethe said, "Boldness has genius, power, and magic in it. Begin it."

There are more ideas, questions, and resources in the appendices. Share your story, and connect to more tools, organizations, and people to help you make a pivot in your life, at www.paulshoemaker.org.

My Family, Where It All Starts . . . and Ends

One of the most meaningful parts of writing this was how many times something reminded me of one of my boys or Lori. My oldest, Ben, is one of the most grounded, solid human beings I've ever known. Yes, I'm biased, but I'm biased about all of the people in my family. Ben is connected to who he is at his core; he knows who he is and he is grounded in it. You can feel it when you are with him.

When he is motivated, my middle son, Nick, is determined like no one else I know. And the optimism that goes along with it is often of the gritty, I'm-gonna-make-this-happen kind. You can feel it when you're around him; it draws you in.

And Sam, my youngest, is so humble, so selfless in his 14-year-old way. There is a kindness and authenticity to his spirit that just oozes out of him and reminds me to strive to have the same kind of humility every time I'm around him. What a gift he gives me.

I can't wait to see who and what each of them continues to become. Each of them is now part of my core. Like me, the boys all need to be better listeners and surely, life has hard places ahead for them. But I have a deep faith in how they will make their way through to a better place, a meaningful life.

And, quite simply, Lori is the biggest can't not do in my life. Corny? Yes. True? Once I fell in love with her, there was no way I was gonna let her go. No way. Marrying Lori was the best answer to *any* question I ever asked in my life.

■ ■ ■

Back in May of last year, my 12-year old boy, Sam, started reading *The Dangerous Book for Boys*.[3] Sam really liked the chapter about building a tree house, and he sat down next to me one evening to tell me a few things about that chapter. The subtle sell job was on. I'll be honest, it didn't take a whole lot for me to sign on. That said, if I had known how many hours it was really going to take, I might not have started. Just a few boards, nails, maybe a few screws and voila, right?

I also know Sam and myself well enough to know that we'd butt heads more than once, but we would keep going—after we either both cooled down or one of us came to his senses. It was clear, very quickly, that there was no way one of us could pull this off on his own, especially since you start six feet above the ground and go up from there.

We pulled together all the necessary items and started hauling them up into a tree in our backyard. We managed to build up and out, with plenty of scrapes and missteps along the way. It was a team effort. Sam made a great general contractor, which left me providing a good deal of the labor. Lori, Nick, and Griffey, our dog, provided consulting and advising expertise from the ground. Honestly, it felt sort of makeshift and flimsy while we were building it.

But the coolest thing about building that tree house was that moment when we bolted the final two corner pieces together. Suddenly, the fairly wobbly structure was darn near solid as a rock. You couldn't push the walls over if you had to. I'm still slightly amazed when I look at it up the tree behind our home. I barely got a C in physics at Iowa State so engineering is not my strength.

Our family building that tree house reminds me of this change-the-world work, albeit on a much smaller scale. Sam was determined and I knew at my core that it would be a meaningful, if not always happy, experience for the two of us. Lori kept reminding me, it's the process, not the result. We were in some hard places, physically and mentally. And there were many times that I had to swallow my dad pride and listen to my young son tell me I was doing it wrong. He had the book so he had the answers and he has an engineer's mind. The whole family connected with the project and everyone got into the spirit of being a "dangerous boy" once we got going. We couldn't not build this tree house.

Whether you find it in a tree house or at a community meeting or an orphanage in Ecuador or in a prison or somewhere else in your life, I hope you will go on this journey with me to find your can't not do. A better world waits for you and a better, more meaningful life awaits you.

APPENDIX INTRODUCTION

My main motivation for writing this book is not just to get your attention and hopefully provide inspiration, but also to motivate and provide pathways for action, to get you going on and advance your can't not do in life. To do, not just think; to act, not just plan. To that end, what follows are a collection of tools, questions, ideas, and resources to help you do just that.

—Paul S.

Please go to www.paulshoemaker.org and share your own stories and resources to help others on this journey—and to find more resources and ideas to help you on your own journey.

20 Questions for a Personal Checklist

Finding Your Focus

I've pulled out the key points from Part I—Finding Your Focus. Your answers will become a sort of personal can't-not-do checklist. Keep your list and periodically revisit it; maybe write your answers down in a journal or on a whiteboard and look them over periodically. This is not rocket science or some mysterious process. It's about people doing the hard, purposeful, intentional work to figure out their can't not do for social change.

Give it some of the same kind of (well, almost) intentionality you may have already given to your career or life mate or how you raise your family or your values in life. I think many of these can be adapted to and discussed at your place of work as well. If you use the questions below, you will paint a picture, a collage that will greatly increase your chances of not only having a more positive impact on the world but on your life too.

What Are You a Determined Optimist About?

1. You only need one can't not do at a time in your life, if you want to have true, sustained impact. Just one. Take a look at the different causes, fundraisers, events, discussions, and volunteer efforts in which you have participated. Google "social issues" if you need a few inventories or lists. Does anything stand out? What is it?

2. You might find out what you are a determined optimist about as the result of a big epiphany or a significant, single event in your life. Or it might be something that emerges over many years. Can you pinpoint the origin? Why is this issue so important to you?

3. Make sure that that you haven't chosen this cause because it is an obligation of some sort instead of something that you are passionate about—want to versus should do. Optimism feeds your passion and rejuvenates your energy far more effectively than duty. Are there underlying issues or hidden agendas or obligations influencing your decision?

4. Your optimism must be grounded in reality. You have a plan or are part of a group that has one and you have strategies that will make real progress on that plan. Do you think you know what works effectively? Are you willing to research or work with people who have a plan and deeper knowledge than you?

5. You must be flexible and resilient. You have a belief in the endgame but know that these problems are enormously complex and involve constant change. Do you know what your end goal looks like? What will success look like in 10 or more years? Do you have an "eyes on the prize" determination to stick with this issue for the long haul and be energized by meeting milestones along the way? Do you look at the complex and entrenched problem and think, "This is hard, but we will find a solution." Do you believe this issue is solvable?

6. Your "cause" might also be a personal or professional expertise (vs. a social problem) you feel you can offer to help. Maybe

you're not passionate about one social problem. But what gifts do you have to offer your community? What expertise and experiences have you spent years building that you are eager and willing to put to work?

7. Your endeavor doesn't have to be full-time or involve a career change. When you think about the cause, how do you see yourself fitting into the solution? Can you sustain your focus over many years?

Who Are You at Your Core?

8. Look at your roots. Trace back through the early years of your life. Think about the people who made you who you are today. What kinds of things did you talk about as a family that you remember most vividly? What teachers, friends, relatives, parents influenced you the most and why? What did you most admire (or not) about the people who influenced your life?

9. Look back through your adult years. What experiences do you clearly remember along the way that have had the greatest effect on who you are today? Are there common themes and threads that bring you to a certain issue or cause?

10. Think about the future. What issue affects you in the most visceral, instinctual way? What sends that chill up your spine? What really grabs your heart, as well as your head?

11. Assess your skills and knowledge. Look at your commitment to an issue just like you would a new job or a new team. What landing spot would best use your skills, experiences, and talents?

12. Talk to others. Ask them what defines you. Make sure you talk with several people who know you through different experiences and vantage points. Take notes. Ask for feedback. Are there patterns or reflections that emerge? Are there any surprises that come out of your conversations?

13. As you talk to others, ask them for feedback about yourself, but also ask how they might think about can't not do for their own lives. What can you learn about your core from listening to someone else?

What Are You Willing to Go through Hard Places For?

14. Think about your mindset and your determination. When you think about the questions above, are you willing to walk through the fire for your cause (or to put your gifts and expertise to work) and keep on going? Is "failure not an option"?

15. You will learn and be changed by your experiences. Are you just as excited about learning as you are about contributing? Are you open-minded or do you have your mind made up?

16. Before you find that cause that you really want to dig into deeply, take inventory. What's going on in your life, your work, and your relationships? Do you have the capacity, right now, to invest a certain number of hours a week and commit some amount of personal energy and emotion for the long term?

17. If you've decided you are ready to dig in to that hard place, think about how and who will support and replenish your energy. Have a personal support plan. Who will be your trusted allies? Who will you turn to who will listen? What will get you through the darkest moments and re-inspire you?

18. You are going fail. It is part of the experience. What have you learned from failures in your life that inform the pathway you want to take toward your can't not do in the future? How did you persevere before and how might that knowledge and wisdom serve you in this work to keep going when things get messy, complex, hard?

19. If you haven't yet felt some pain and hardship, you are almost certainly not close enough to the real problems to effect and be a

part of real change. What are those hardships you might face? How would they affect your determination?

20. Please spend some time thinking about what is meaningful versus what makes you happy. They aren't necessarily contradictory. How will your answers guide the direction you take?

20 Suggestions for a Personal Checklist

How You Do This Work Well

C hapters 4–6 are all about how you show up and put your can't not do into action. Those three chapters about humility, listening, and connecting are what make you and your can't not do most effective once you've defined it in chapters 1–3. Consider this a list of 20 pointers or best practices to think about to help guide you in your work.

Humility

1. Authentically humble people, regular heroes, have a sort of egoless quality, a willingness to be vulnerable, to ask for help, to say "I don't know."
2. Being deeply authentic and vulnerable builds trust, respect, and safety.
3. You have to know and embrace that you are going to be put in uncomfortable positions and hard places where you will not be in control. Be ready to be vulnerable.

4. Humility, or lack of it, probably shows up more intensely and influences more outcomes in philanthropy, than it does just about anywhere else in our lives. Be extra mindful: you need to practice "humility on steroids."

5. It's hard to overstate how meaningful this "I deserve it" versus "I was lucky" mindset about money and power is. The reality of the answer doesn't matter nearly as much as your perception, the true lens through which you see the world.

6. Humility in the name of only doing so much or worrying about offending someone when the truth will have greater impact is not much better than arrogance.

Listening

7. Study, absorb, understand, try to get the whole situation and all its complexity and nuances. You can't make the gray world of social progress black and white.

8. Ask questions before telling answers as often as possible.

9. When you listen to someone describe a challenge or a solution, you allow her to think through the challenges, possible solutions, and outcomes for herself. She often knows the answer; she just needs to say it out loud and have someone actively listen.

10. The people that you listen to become your trusted allies over time.

11. Understand the difference between position power and referent power you learned about in Management 101. With the former, you are the leader and people follow because they *have* to; with the latter, you are the leader and more people follow because they *want* to.

Connecting

12. It's only by listening and asking questions that you can be a great connector.

13. Consider connecting people even though, at the time, you don't know what will end up happening.

14. You might be a connector/leader from the front of the pack, from the back of the parade, or walking alongside. You might be a servant leader or use your own bully pulpit when it's needed.

15. It's about dogged, stubborn persistence. Nothing sexy, just keep at it. In my work to get people connected into SVP, so far the longest time it's taken to get someone to join our network is 11 years.

16. Keep track of every person (okay, maybe 98 percent) with whom you come in contact. You need to have a database, literally, where you keep track of them, the notes on your conversations, anything and everything. You never know which person you talked to X years ago will become the key missing link tomorrow.

17. Keep in contact with as many people as you can with some regularity. Even if, for many, it's just the occasional e-mail, text, or note to keep the connection going; it's worth it.

18. When the connection drops because you've lost track of the person or their contact information, remember we live in a world of social media. More often than not, one of your friends knows where the person went or how to find them today. If you work hard enough, there's almost no one you can't find via LinkedIn, Google, or Facebook.

19. Connect at the heart, not just the head, level. There are facts and figures that connect us, but more than anything, stories and hearts connect us for the long haul.

20. Whenever you meet someone or are in a meeting or room with other people, stop and think who else should this person, these people, be connected to? Just make it a habit.

■ ■ ■

Please go to www.paulshoemaker.org and share your own stories and resources to help others on this journey—and to find more resources and ideas to help you on your own journey!

APPENDIX 3

Which Stories Fit You Best?

I t's important that you can relate closely to some of these personal stories. I think you can learn *something* from *all* of the stories but there may be some that are more relevant, based on:

How Much Effort and Time You Can Put In
- Full-time: Lisa Chin (Chapter 2), Vu Le (Chapter 2), Heidi Breeze-Harris (Chapter 7)
- Part-time: Kevin Shaw (Chapter 4), Paul Gross (Chapter 7), Bill Henningsgaard (Chapter 5), David Griffis (Chapter 6)
- A Few Hours a Week: Kerry McLenahan (Chapter 1), Dwight Frindt (Chapter 1), Suzi Levine (Chapter 6)

Whether You Are Motivated by International Causes or Social Challenges Closer to Home
- International Focus: Heidi (Chapter 7), Dwight (Chapter 1), Eric Stowe (Chapter 1)
- Domestic/U.S. Focus: Kerry (Chapter 1), Eleuthera Lisch (Chapter 3), Jeff Tollefson (Chapter 4)

Whether Your Can't Not Do Is about a Specific Social Issue versus a Personal Passion or Expertise

- Social Issue: Connie Ballmer (Chapter 3), Eric (Chapter 1), David Risher (Chapter 1)
- Personal Expertise or Passion: Kevin (Chapter 4), Griff (Chapter 6), Bill (Chapter 5)

How You Came to Realize Your Can't Not Do

- Had an Epiphany: David (Chapter 1), Lisa (Chapter 2), Heidi (Chapter 7)
- Took a Longer Road to Determine: Eric (Chapter 1), Kevin (Chapter 4), Vu (Chapter 2)

Additional Resources for Getting Started

SVP Stuff, Books, Websites, and Blogs

For each book, I've also noted the associated questions from Appendix 1 that I believe it's most relevant to.

SVP Stuff

The whole network: www.socialventurepartners.org
SVP Seattle: www.socialventurepartners.org/seattle
What we do: www.socialventurepartners.org/seattle/what-we-do/
Why it matters: www.socialventurepartners.org/seattle/why-it-matters/
To join, click on where we are at: www.socialventurepartners.org
Some great stories: www.socialventurepartners.org/seattle/news-events/
    stories/

Books

Arrillaga-Andreesen, Laura. 2012. *Giving 2.0*. San Francisco, CA: Jossey-Bass. Q3, 7

Behar, Howard. 2007. *It's Not about the Coffee*. New York, NY: Penguin Group.

Bornstein, David. 2007. *How to Change the World*. Oxford, United Kingdom: Oxford University Press. Q2, Q6

Brown, Brene. 2012. *Daring Greatly*. Rutherford, NJ: Gotham Books. Q3, 7, 9, 10, 18.

Chartavian, Gerald. 2012. *A Year Up*. New York, NY: Penguin Group. Q5

Collins, Jim. 2005. *Good to Great and the Social Sector*. New York, NY: Harper Collins. Q15

Coyle, Daniel. 2009. *The Talent Code*. New York, NY: Bantam Dell. Q11, 16

Crutchfield, Leslie, John Kania, and John Kramer. 2011. *Do More Than Give*. San Francisco, CA: Jossey-Bass. Q5

Duarte, Nancy. 2010. *Resonate*. Hoboken, NJ: John Wiley & Sons.

Eggers, Robert. 2013. *The Social Revolution*. New York, NY: Deloitte Touche Tohamatsu. Q1, 11

Emerson, Jed. 2015. *The Impact Investor*. Hoboken, NJ: John Wiley & Sons.

Gary, Tracy. 2008. *Inspired Philanthropy*. San Francisco, CA: Jossey-Bass. Q1

Gladwell, Malcolm. 2000. *The Tipping Point*. New York, NY: Little, Brown & Co.

Godin, Seth. 2008. *Tribes* and *What to Do When It's Your Turn*. New York, NY: Penguin Group. Q9, 10

Goodman, Andy. 2009. *Storytelling as Best Practice*. Los Angeles, CA: The Goodman Center.

Hammond, Darrell. *Kaboom*. Emmaus, PA: Rodale Books, Q8

Hurst, Aaron. 2014. *The Purpose Economy*. Boise, ID: Elevate. Q20

Kristof, Nick, and Sheryl Wu Dunn. 2014. *A Path Appears*. New York, NY: Random House. Q4, 14, 19

McLeod Grant, Heather, and Leslie Crutchfield, *Forces for Good*. San Francisco, CA: Jossey-Bass. Q4, 5

Morino, Mario. 2011. *Leap of Reason*. Washington, DC: Morino Institute. Q14, 15

Myckoskie, Blake. 2011. *Start Something That Matters*. New York, NY: Random House. Q1, 11

Norton, Lisa. 2012. *How to Be a Global Nonprofit*. Hoboken, NJ: John Wiley & Sons.

Palotta, Dan. 2008. *Uncharitable*. Medford, MA: Tufts University Press.

Pink, Daniel. 2009. *Drive*. New York, NY: Riverhead Books. Q11

Putnam, Robert. 2000. *Bowling Alone* and *Better Together*. New York, NY: Simon & Schuster.

Ryan, Bill and Richard Chait. 2005. *Governance as Leadership*. Hoboken, NJ: John Wiley & Sons.

Sachs, Jonas. 2012. *Winning the Story Wars*. Boston, MA: Harvard Business School Publishing.

Tierney, Tom. 2011. *Give Smart*. New York, NY: Public Affairs Books. Q1, 15

Twist, Lynne. 2000. *The Soul of Money*. New York, NY: W.W. Norton & Co. Q13

Warren, Rick. 2002. *The Purpose-Driven Life*. Grand Rapids, MI: Zondervan. Q2, 10, 16

Wheatley, Meg. *A Simpler Way*. 1996. Oakland, CA: Berrett-Koehler Publishers. Q12

Websites

Net Impact, www.netimpact.org

Volunteer Match, www.volunteermatch.org

Points of Light/HandsOn Network, www.handsonnetwork.org

Blueprints for Healthy Youth Development – www.blueprintsprograms
.com

Grantmakers for Effective Organizations, www.geofunders.org

Center on Wealth and Philanthropy, Boston College, www.bc.edu/
research/cwp.html

New Profit Inc – www.newprofit.com

Venture Philanthropy Partners – www.vppartners.org

American Leadership Forum – www.alfnational.org

Seattle Works, www.seattleworks.org

The Seattle Foundation, www.seattlefoundation.org

Social Development Research Group, www.sdrg.org

Edna McConnell Clark Foundation, www.emcf.org

Robin Hood Foundation, www.robinhood.org

MDRC, www.mdrc.org

Bridgespan, www.bridgespan.org

FSG, FSG.org

Blogs

Seth Godin, www.sethgodin.com

Inside Philanthropy, www.insidephilanthropy.com

Stanford Social Innovation Review, www.ssireview.org

Nonprofit with Balls, www.nonprofitwithballs.com

Chapter-by-Chapter Summary

Prologue: The Power of Can't Not Do

"I can't not do this." "It's not that I can do this, it's that I can't not. I don't have time to not make an impact." "I could not imagine not." I don't remember the first person I heard use one of these grammatically incorrect phrases. You've heard of can-do people, but the regular heroes you will meet in this book go way beyond "can do." They can't not do. They make a decision—at some point in their lives—that there is something, some burning issue, that they can't not do something about. There is a reason, a power, in why they say "can't not do." These people have found a cause that grabbed them and wouldn't let go. It made them dig deeper and find the conviction and dedication to jump into the issue for the long haul.

Introduction: Why Our Social Drives Matter More Now—The Multipliers

Far more than ever before, in the past 10 to 20 years, just a few people can do so much. Advances in technology, connectedness, and globalization are converging to become *force multipliers* that can either increase the magnitude of our social problems or accelerate the solutions to them. The concept of force multipliers refers to a combination of attributes that make a given force more effective than that same force would be without those attributes. These forces for social progress (or decline) are at an historic tipping point. With a growing sense of urgency, we ultimately need more committed people to become the difference makers driving and utilizing these social multipliers for positive change, tipping the balance toward a better world.

Chapter 1 David Risher, the Lost Key and Eradicating Illiteracy: *Are You a Determined Optimist?*

If you're going to dive into this change-the-world business, you better believe that solving the problem at hand is possible. Can we eradicate illiteracy in the developing world (and at home)? Can we end homelessness? World hunger? Determined optimists are people who believe a solution to a given social challenge is possible—they are hard-core problem solvers who do not believe "no" is a viable answer. Determined optimists see "their" social challenge as a puzzle to be solved, not a hopelessly entrenched problem. Optimism is a necessity for can't-not-do work because of its exceptional power to spur action and inspire others, but most important, to provide the fuel to burn when the challenges seem greatest and determination is needed most.

Chapter 2 Lisa Chin Is Not Doing This to Be Happy: *Who Are You at Your Core?*

Core beliefs are fundamental to who you are, to what you truly see and aspire to in yourself and in your world. They form the internal compass that guides you. The idea of your work, your cause, being connected to your core is about optimizing what you are good at and what plays to your talents and passions most intensely. When your one cause is connected to and resonates with your core beliefs, you will give more to it more freely, you will more easily dedicate effort and time, and, ultimately, you and others will earn greater reward. Time matters. Lives can be saved and enriched. The sooner the right cause finds you, the sooner you can make a long-term commitment and the more good you can achieve. A simple four-question evaluation—based on years of experience observing successful and unsuccessful change makers—can assist you in exploring and affirming what is at your core.

Chapter 3 Eleuthera Lisch, Stepping Out from behind the Fourth Wall: *Are You Willing to Go to Hard Places?*

When you have dug into what you believe you can't not do, the hard places are sure to follow—where you find the real challenges, meet the real people, and confront the unpredictability of the our world. It is where your commitment to can't not do is tested. Can you be effective when the going gets tough? Can you persevere despite the odds and the foes? Each successful change agent I talked with knew with certainty that digging deeply into this work will sometimes be very hard, but they also knew that the hard places are *the* place where real change happens. And what do you do with those moments where you encounter the proverbial storm and feel like you have lost everything? As would-be change agents, we need to reconstruct our relationship to failure and rethink the role it plays in helping to make us better, stronger, more effective people. Without the willingness to fail, which is what will at times inevitably happen when we dig into the hard places of social change, substantial change will not occur.

Chapter 4 Jeff Tollefson, Losing It All and Becoming Richer: *Are You Ready to Be Humble and Humbled?*

This is all about deeds, not words. Words don't mean jack when it comes to the kind of authentic, powerful humility that makes change happen. Humility is a critical ingredient in achieving greater impact in this change-the-world work. Authentically humble people have a sort of egoless quality, an openness to others, and a willingness to ask for help and say "I don't know." I'll call it humility on steroids and when you're around it, it stands out . . . or not. You also have to be willing to *be* humbled, to put your ego at risk and be vulnerable. You have to know and embrace that you are going to be put in uncomfortable positions (hard places) where you will not be in control or where you might appear foolish. This is not easy stuff. It's easier to try to help your community in ways that feel good and light-hearted. But, by playing it safe you won't find what you are truly capable of and won't be able to move the needle of change on really tough issues. Being humbled is transformative. Great change agents will go "find" the humility in this work, meaning it may not find you if you resist circumstances in which you might be humbled. This work is neither for the faint-hearted nor for the big egos that can't accept more than one dose of humility. If you don't get humbled more than once, you're still on the sidelines.

Chapter 5 Lori, I Got Married a Little too Early to the Right Woman: *Can You Actively Listen?*

Being a great listener is one of the most powerful assets a person can possess. Do you study, absorb, process, and try to understand the whole situation and all its complexity and nuances? You can't make the gray world of social progress black and white. You just can't. When you *actively* listen, you can hear, feel, and see all the gray. You have to; you can't not. If you are a truly deep listener, you will have more power to do good than through almost any other attribute you could possess. Every time you listen deeply and authentically, you do a little more to create another leader for the cause. You help other people see their personal power; you don't just create more leaders but more *effective* leaders around you. You engender a level of trust and relationship in people around you who will serve you through the hard times, values that are surely needed in the journey to create positive change. And you become more powerful, in every good sense of the word, because your words count for more and you've *empowered* more and more people.

Chapter 6 Suzi Levine, Learning When Not to Raise Her Hand: *Do You Believe 1 + 1 = 3?*

Successful social change agents have to be connectors of the parts and people of this work as much and as often as they can. If you want to effect change, you can't just own or solve stuff by yourself. This work requires that you are motivated, even hungry, to connect to the right people and to connect the right people with each other, even when they don't look, act, or behave like you. A lot of what we've talked about so far are the qualities and mindset an individual needs to possess or assume to do this work. But an equally powerful tool is connecting networks of individuals and other passionate people. Networks are everywhere in our lives, but we've just scratched the surface of the power of networks to tackle our toughest social challenges. When you connect your internal potential and passion to networks, you can go so much further, faster—together. It's a virtuous cycle. Those relationships with others will, in turn, impact what's inside each of us and strengthen our internal foundation.

Chapter 7 Heidi Breeze-Harris, a Sick Pregnant Lady with an Idea: *What Is Your Can't Not Do?*

You will either find this can't-not-do feeling or you won't, and it might not be now or yet, but I sure hope it will be someday for each of you. Because it changes your life in creative, deep, rewarding ways you could never imagine. It is what gets you out of bed, off the sidelines, and into the action. It is the catalyst to achieve your potential to change our world. The change agents I've worked with have told me that to not do what they are doing would be criminal, cowardly, and that "they'd be a charade." There is a sense of being compelled to do the good work they are endeavoring to do. Even when that work calls them to face, absorb, and overcome challenges at home and around the world that they've never dealt with before. It becomes part of who they are, their identity, and someday a part of their legacy. Not in a burdensome way, but rather, it gives people a more expansive, forwarded-thinking self-image. It's impossible to overstate how much greater impact each of us, all of us, would have if we found our can't not do in life and focused our time and resources there.

Chapter 8 Why Our Social Drives Matter More Now: *The Equation*

It's not a lack of solutions or funding that is primarily holding our schools or communities back. The simple facts are these: (1) we have solutions to many social challenges, far more than most people think, and (2) we have a significant amount of financial resources to invest in ameliorating those challenges. Combine those two facts with the more recent dynamics we discussed in Chapter 1 about social multipliers, and we now have just about everything we need to make significant social progress in the next generation: *Known Solutions + Financial Resources + Social Multipliers = Significant Social Progress!*

Those three factors in that equation are forces, just waiting to be focused . . . and if not focused, they dissipate and are wasted, which happens far too often. Why doesn't that equation add up often enough in our communities and ecosystems? The answer is almost inescapable and it's what this whole book has been about. This book is full of stories of can't-not-do people who ultimately converged and focused those three elements in a way that created significant, break-the-norm positive social progress.

Conclusion: Surrendering to the Intention

This work to help change the world isn't a one-way street; when you really dig in, it's two-way, purpose-infusing, and ultimately positive. Being a determined optimist, connecting to your core self, going to hard places, being humble and humbled, being an active listener and a connector will most surely impact the can't not do you are or will become so passionate about. The impact of a new wave of socially minded change agents, like you, in our future society has the potential to make a profound difference in our communities and around the world. In the next 50 years, the same kind of progress we've seen made in the past 50—on social issues like teen pregnancy and violent crime—is now possible for education, the environment, better standards of living, and more.

NOTES

Prologue

1. The lab is the Institute for Learning & Brain Sciences (I-LABS). It is an interdisciplinary center dedicated to discovering the fundamental principles of human learning, with special emphasis on children ages 0 to 5. It is the world's first brain-imaging facility focused on children.

2. www.laalmanac.com/crime/cr03x.htm.

3. www.psmag.com/politics-and-law/the-end-of-gangs-los-angeles-southern-california-epidemic-crime-95498.

4. 2015 Gates Annual Letter, Bill & Melinda Gates Foundation.

Introduction

1. http://magazine.jhsph.edu/2003/fall/SARS/.

2. According to the Department of Defense, a force multiplier is defined as a capability that, when added to and employed by a combat force, significantly increases the combat potential of that force and thus enhances the probability of successful mission accomplishment. Today the term is also applied more broadly, to refer to nonmilitary-related situations, such as cases in business, sports, and social issues.

3. Claudia Rowe, "Teachers Jump-Start a Turnaround," *Seattle Times* October 26, 2013.

4. Ibid.

5. In addition to drawing from my conversation with Dr. Reece, some of the facts here are from www.seattletimes.com/seattle-news/teachers-jump-start-turnaround-at-white-center-heights-elementary/.

6. www.plexusinstitute.org/blogpost/656763/189550/Emergent-Strategies-for-Complex-Social-Systems.

7. https://www.youtube.com/watch?v=jJgpU66T6Ns.

8. DNAinfo New York, April 8, 2014: www.dnainfo.com/new-york/20140408/richmond-hill/nypds-compstat-creator-jack-maple-may-have-street-renamed-after-him.

9. www.imdb.com/title/tt0268978/.

10. "Homicide Data since 1963," www.NYC.gov. Blue Room press release, "Mayor Bloomberg and Police Commissioner Kelly Announce 2012 Sets All-time Record for Fewest Murders and Fewest Shootings in New York City History," December 28, 2012.

Chapter 1 David Risher, the Lost Key, and Eradicating Illiteracy

1. "Adult and Youth Literacy," UNESCO Institute for Statistics Fact Sheet no. 26, September 2013.

2. https://www.youtube.com/watch?v=nmO22xzHFqg.

3. Eric Stowe, "'40 Under 40' Honoree," *Puget Sound Business Journal,* September 14, 2012.

4. Angela Lee Duckworth, "The Key to Success? Grit," TED Talks Education, April 2013, www.ted.com/talks/angela_lee_duckworth_the_key_to_success_grit?language=en.

5. www.ascd.org/publications/educational-leadership/sept13/vol71/num01/The-Significance-of-Grit@-A-Conversation-with-Angela-Lee-Duckworth.aspx.

Chapter 2 Lisa Chin Is Not Doing This to Be Happy

1. There's a great two-minute explanation of "opportunity youth" at www.yearup.org/stories/finding-opportunity/.

Chapter 3 Eleuthera Lisch, Stepping Out from Behind the Fourth Wall

1. Daniel Coyle, *The Talent Code: Greatness Isn't Born. It's Grown. Here's How* (New York: Bantam Books, 2009).

2. www.mayoclinic.org/diseases-conditions/post-traumatic-stress-disorder/basics/definition/con-20022540.

3. https://www.childwelfare.gov/topics/systemwide/statistics/childwelfare-foster/?hasBeenRedirected=1.

4. Girls Rock! is a 10-week rock-climbing course aimed at building inquisitive courage in middle school age girls. Each week they meet with their group and mentors to learn the fundamentals of rock climbing, problem solving, and trust while climbing indoors. During the fifth week the girls participate in an overnight, outdoor rock-climbing trip with the program culminating in a celebratory graduation where the girls share what they have learned with friends and family. In 2011, Metrocenter YMCA reported 98 percent of participants identified ways they could use the courage skills they learned in the program in real life, and 79 percent report having more courage to raise their hand and answer a question in class. One hundred percent of participants said they learned to trust someone in the program.

5. http://faculty-gsb.stanford.edu/aaker/pages/documents/somekeydifferenceshappylifemeaningfullife_2012.pdf.

Chapter 4 Jeff Tollefson, Losing It All and Becoming Richer

1. Elizabeth Svoboda, *What Makes a Hero? The Surprising Science of Selflessness* (London: Penguin Books, 2013).

2. I wrote a blog post on this at www.ssireview.org/blog/entry/reconstructing_philanthropy_from_the_outsidein.

3. http://www.ssireview.org/blog/entry/reconstructing_philanthropy_from_the_outsidein

4. Tom Peters, *In Search of Excellence* (New York: Harper Collins, 1984, 2002).

5. www.ted.com/talks/brene_brown_on_vulnerability.

6. Thomas Friedman, "How to Get a Job at Google," *New York Times*, February 22, 2014.

7. www.jimcollins.com/books.html.

8. Bo Burlingham, "The Re-Education of Jim Collins," *Inc.*, October 2014.

Chapter 5 Lori, I Got Married a Little Too Early to the *Right* Woman

1. Stephen Covey, *The 7 Habits of Highly Effective People* (New York: Free Press, a division of Simon & Schuster, 1989 and 2004).

2. Annie M. Paul, "The Power of Smart Listening," *Time*, December 11, 2011.

3. www.speakingaboutpresenting.com/presentation-myths/mehrabian-nonverbal-communication-research/.

4. Ernesto Sirolli, "Want to Help Someone? Shut Up and Listen!" TEDx Christchurch, September 2012.

5. Mike Myatt, *Hacking Leadership: The 11 Gaps Every Business Needs to Close and the Secrets to Closing Them Quickly* (Hoboken, NJ: John Wiley & Sons, 2013).

6. Daniel Ames, Lily Benjamin Maissen, and Joel Brockner, "The Role of Listening in Interpersonal Influence," *Journal of Research in Personality* 46 (February 2012): 345–349.

Chapter 6 Suzi Levine, Learning When Not to Raise Her Hand

1. A. Gopnic, A., A.N. Meltzoff, and P.K. Kuhl, *The Scientist in the Crib: What Early Learning Tells Us about the Mind* (New York: William Morrow Paperbacks, 2000).

2. www.socialventurepartners.org/seattle/2012/03/26/breaking-the-rules-changing-the-world/.

3. Deborah Gordon, "The Emergent Genius of Ant Colonies" (Monterey, CA: TED2003), https://www.ted.com/talks/deborah_gordon_digs_ants.

4. Margaret J. Wheatley, *A Simpler Way* (San Francisco: Berrett-Koehler Publishers, 1998).

5. http://en.wikipedia.org/wiki/Metcalfe's_law.

6. Kevin Kelly, *New Rules for the New Economy* (London: Penguin Books, 1999).

7. Malcolm Gladwell, *The Tipping Point: How Little Things Can Make a Big Difference* (New York: Back Bay Books, 2002).

8. Seth Godin, *Tribes: We Need You to Lead Us* (New York: Portfolio Hardcover, 2008).

Chapter 8 Why *Your* Social Drives Matter More New

1. David Kirp, *Improbable Scholars* (New York: Oxford University Press, 2013).

2. www.ted.com/talks/peter_diamandis_abundance_is_our_future?language=en.

3. http://ncrp.org/publications?p=product&id=3.

Conclusion

1. http://faculty-gsb.stanford.edu/aaker/pages/documents/somekeydifferenceshappylifemeaningfullife_2012.pdf

2. http://newsroom.ucla.edu/releases/don-t-worry-be-happy-247644.

3. Conn Iggulden and Hal Iggulden, *The Dangerous Book for Boys,* U.S. edition (New York: William Morrow, 2012).

ABOUT THE AUTHOR

Paul Shoemaker has been SVP Seattle's executive connector for 17 years. Anyone who's met him knows why. If you're out to change the world, he's there to connect you to the people and organizations on that same journey.

Paul is committed to working in the community, serving on the boards of several organizations. He is the founding president of Social Venture Partners International and currently sits on its board of directors, as well as the board of Partners for Our Children. Past work includes a term as board treasurer of Grantmakers for Effective Organizations (2001–2007), as well as board service for the Microsoft Alumni Foundation (2008–2013), Children's Alliance in Seattle (1996–2000), and Treepeople in Los Angeles (1987–1990).

In 2011 and 2012, Paul was named one of the Top 50 Most Influential People in the Non-Profit Sector by *The NonProfit Times*. In 2013, he received the Red Winged Leadership Award from Seattle University's Albers School of Business and Economics and the Philanthropist of the Year Award from Future in Review. In 2014, he was named a Rockefeller Foundation Bellagio Fellow. He has appeared in numerous media including NBC, CBS, *Fortune* magazine, *Bloomberg News*, and many others. He has spoken at the 2013 Social Good Summit, 2012 TEDxRainier, 2015 TEDxFargo and dozens of other social sector conferences over the years.

Before coming to SVP Seattle in 1998, Paul was group manager for worldwide operations at Microsoft Corporation and developed a group of 22 direct marketing professionals and implemented a direct marketing infrastructure. Prior to his work at Microsoft, Paul was a product manager at Nestlé USA in Glendale, California. Paul holds an MBA in marketing and finance from the University of Texas and a BBA in accounting from Iowa State University. Paul enjoys life with his wife and three sons, and is an avid sports fan, especially of his own kids' teams, as well as the Seattle Seahawks (why didn't they just hand the ball to Marshawn on the one-yard line?!), and pursues his hobby as a high school basketball referee.

ACKNOWLEDGMENTS

When you write a section like this, it's almost unnerving because of the thought of missing someone, just one important person. So if I've missed anyone, I'm sorry and you have my deepest thanks! The people I know I need to thank for sure include everyone in this book; you made this book possible and my life so much richer; Bettijean Collins, my amazing editor and no-BS friend; Heidi Toboni at Helt Consulting, who guided me through this process so smartly and surely; Matt Davis at John Wiley & Sons and Mark Fortier at Fortier PR, who helped make this happen out in the world; Paul and Debbi Brainerd, Scott Oki, Maggie and Doug Walker, Ida Cole, Bill Neukom, the founders of SVP, none of this exists without your vision and friendship; Erin Kahn, Aaron Jacobs, Rona Pryor, Tom Donlea, Susan Fairchild, Ruth Jones, Azania Andrews, Heidi Winterkorn Craemer, Marie Sauter, Sofia Michelakis, Lynn Coriano, Sally Gillis, Mike Quinn, Marlene Rapues, Megan Bartot, Becca Stephens, Ben Mitchell, and Juliet Le, all of the awesome SVP and SVPI staff that have been along for this amazing journey; Keith Kegley and Larry Fox, two of the most thoughtful "thought partners" anyone could ever hope for; truth-teller friends Will Novy-Hilldeseley, Ben Klasky, Nancy Cannon, Lynann Bradbury, Dawn Trudeau, Fraser Black, and Chris Rogers, you have no idea how much I value each of you; SVP International board members over the years, too many to list all of them, but you all made the collective so much more than anyone ever thought possible, especially Brad Zumwalt, Bob Wright, Lance Fors,

John Fort, Dan Catlin, Denis Cavner, Alan Sorkin, Andy and Krystyna Williamson, Hideki Inoue, and Kevin Shaw. Thank you, Jerry Hirsch, for being the first guy to make SVP into more than one city and a friend of the highest degree ever since; so many partners at SVP Seattle, it's literally impossible to list or prioritize them. It would take me another book and a month of my life to thank all of you for everything you have done for this world, this community, and for me. A handful do stand out who have been such mentors and guides in the past year or two: Todd Vogel, Tony LaLiberte, Ron Tanemura, Emily Anthony, Lisa Norton, John Sage, Vanessa Kirsch, Kim Syman, Julie Davis, Charlotte Guyman, Mike and Jackie Bezos, Lowell Weiss, Brian Vowinkel, Mike and Molly Hanlon, Janet Levinger, Tony Mestres, Victor Alcantara, Norm Bontje, Gideon Rosenblatt and CJ Liu—and I know there are a few more I should add, but I don't know where to stop. I'll add Brad Brickman, Austin McNamee, Emer Dooley, Mike Cadigan, and Susan Mitchell, for taking the time to talk to me about this book too; Olivia Leland, John Brown, and Dean Hachamovitch for your feedback and friendship; so many awesome, spectacular colleagues out there in the social sector who informed this book and my beliefs in countless ways. They include: Heather McLeod Grant, Peter Hero, Melinda Tuan, Darrell Hamond, Glen Galaich, Henry Berman, Jed Emerson, Jim Collins, Jim Pitofsky, John Wood, Katherine Fulton, Laura Arrillaga-Andreesen, John Burgess, Richard Woo, Dan Cardinali, Sterling Speirn and Diana Aviv, Tom Tierney and Jeff Bradach, John Kania and Fay Hanley Brown, Ann Krumboltz, Colleen Willoughby, Tricia Raikes, Tricia McKay, Aaron Hurst, Alan Khazei, Andy Goodman, Banny Banerjee, Kathleen Enright, Grant Oliphant, Gregg Behr, Mario Morino, Cheryl Dahle. There are four authors who inspire me all the time: Seth Godin, Daniel Pink, Nick Kristof, and Malcolm Gladwell, plus all of the other authors listed in Appendix 3. I've read and admire all of your work greatly. Thanks also to my first boss, Brad Alford, whom I learned more from than anyone at work other than maybe Dawn

Trudeau; my two referee buddies, Matt Mason and Tim Gately, that are just A-1 human beings and gave me a few great slices of feedback along the way as I wrote this. And to my family back in Iowa: Mom and Dad, Peg and Jim, Mary and Dave, Mark, Jacce, and Aly, Jeff and Keith—thanks for putting up with me all these years. And just one more time—to everyone who was ever an SVP partner, investee, colleague, or community member—there are thousands of you who make this world a better place and have helped me countless times along this journey of my own can't not do in life.

THANK YOU

INDEX